Emotional Victories Systematic Failures

The Only Book Every Financial Advisor Needs To Read

Elias R. Dau, CRPC®

Exigent Publishing

LADERA RANCH, CALIFORNIA

Elias R. Dau/Exigent Publishing
32 Bushwood Circle
Ladera Ranch, California/92694
www.eliasrdau.com

Publisher's Note: This book and the content provided herein are simply for educational purposes and do not take the place of professional advice. Every effort has been made to ensure that the content provided in this book is accurate and helpful for our readers at publishing time. However, this is not an exhaustive treatment of the subjects. No liability is assumed for losses or damages due to the information provided.

Emotional Victories Systematic Failures/ Elias R. Dau. -- 1st ed.
ISBN 978-1-7360440-0-1

I dedicate this book to my wife, three children and my parents for their love, intrepid support and faith in me. You make me strive to be a better man.

I further dedicate this book to the countless leaders and financial advisors that helped me along the way. Without you, this book could not be possible.

"Success isn't just about what you accomplish in your life; it's about what you inspire others to do."
—UNKNOWN

Contents

Acknowledgements

To Phil Sieg, thank you for giving me a role model to look up to and for giving me the best piece of advice in my career, along with all the other advice along the way.

Thank you, Jim Byrne for helping me early on in my business. You had countless young advisors come to you for help and you chose me. You taught me how to remain calm and objective in turbulent markets and for that, I will always be grateful!

To Ron Connors, you gave me my first shot at leadership and trusted me from the beginning of my leadership path. You have been a tremendous advocate and I appreciate it. My family and I are so grateful that our paths crossed, along the way.

Chris, Chuck and Andy — Thank you for your unwavering friendship over the decades. We've taught each other, supported each other and loved each other through thick and thin. Thank you guys.

Erin Tambarella — Thank you for your coaching, pragmatic advice and guidance into a better executive. Thanks also for always holding me accountable while writing this book and helping me to make it a reality.

Introduction

"Don't be afraid to give up the good to go for the great."
— John D. Rockefeller

This book was conceived, and writing began pre-Covid 19. Originally, I started the book by reflecting on how I'd never been more shocked than when I had heard about Kobe Bryant's death. Little did I know that not even 60 days later, I would have the shock of my life as I watched a casual news story out of China grow into a full-blown global pandemic.

Yes, to some of us Kobe was immortal, and his death had a dramatic impact where I live in Orange County, CA. It was felt by almost everyone. In addition to Kobe and Gianna,- six other people perished that day. It seemed like everybody I knew was somehow connected to someone on that flight. Kobe had such an impact not only on the game of basketball but also on the lives of so many people because of his outreach into the community. He changed people's lives. For the days and weeks that followed, I asked myself if I was making an impact on people's lives. I spoke with clients, advisors, peers and asked them the same thing: Is what we do making a positive impact on others? My answer was a resounding *yes*. When done correctly, what we do is a noble profession.

Fast-forward a few short weeks to April 2020 and it seems like everyone I know is connected to someone who is sick with the Coronavirus. My wife works in the Emergency Room so it is a reality for me and my family. Everyone is struggling to navigate their new reality. People are afraid, and the economic implications of shelter-in-place orders that have been effective in every state for an extended period of time is staggering.

No one is quite sure what to expect. We've experienced unprecedented volatility in the markets. Between February and March, we moved from all-time highs to correction territory in record time. In March, the Dow had its worst single day loss in history. The precipitous market drop, which happened so fast and unexpectedly, caught many investors off guard.

I got into the investment business for times like these—times when I could make a real difference in people's lives. Clients and prospects need you more than ever during turbulent times. But, is your business prepared for turbulent times?

The man who got me into the business was a former girlfriend of mine's dad. He had a nice house, travelled the world, drove a nice car, and put his two daughters through college without debt. I asked him how I could do what he did and he introduced me to his local manager. I made my way into the firm.

There wasn't a base salary so I worked for 100% commission and had to earn every dollar. In fact, my very first paycheck was 25 cents. I eventually gained momentum and it looked like this was the career for me. In my third year I was beginning to gain some traction in my business. I won a few sales contests (when they were allowed) and gained some local recognition.

Then, my girlfriend and I went to her parents' house for the weekend and all seemed to be going great. They asked her to run to the store but asked me to stay back. They sat across from me at the kitchen table. Mandy (her mom) had a yellow legal pad with what looked like some sort of list on it. Both of them proceeded to tell me why I would not be successful in this business and encouraged me to get out and to search for a different job. I was shocked. The very person that helped me get into the business wanted me to get out of the business!

It wasn't too long after that conversation that I broke up with her and made it my goal to be as successful as I could be in this business. And that's exactly what I did. I sunk my time and energy into everything I could possibly do to be as successful as possible. I eventually found the love of my life, and she supported me as I grew my business and we now have a beautiful family with three children.

Fast forward, almost a decade and in 2008, while living in New Jersey, the financial world came crashing down around me, my first child was born in July, and my mother was battling cancer. I was driving back and forth between my mother's hospital in Philadelphia and my wife and daughter's hospital in Northern New Jersey.

It was at that time that I realized I needed to position my business in such a way that I would have the capacity to handle life's unexpected moments. 2008 was a year filled with amazing highs and the lowest of lows but that experience was exactly what helped me decide to run my business like a business.

If you're successful in this business, it's because you're good at selling, building relationships, and you are trusted. The problem is that no one ever taught you how to run your business like a business. This is important under normal circumstances, but it can catapult you to higher success or put you on the ropes wondering why you chose this profession.

In volatile markets, people want to know that you are putting their interests first and that you're watching out for their best interests. You can only fly-by-the-seat of your pants for so long. If you want to do your very best for clients and grow in both good times and bad, you must create systems for your business that free up your time and allow you to become more effective in all aspects of your business. This invariably results in more assets, more revenue, and more referrals.

Think of the businesses you frequent: your favorite restaurant, hotel, or resort. You probably love these places and keep going back because they're consistent. The food is always fantastic, the beds are always comfortable, and the service is always outstanding. Consistency is the mark of a great business, but consistency doesn't just happen in those businesses or yours.

Consistency in your business means clients can count on you to do what you say you will do. They get meaningful and consistent contact from you because you have a system for that and when times are volatile, client contact increases because you have a system for that, too.

Premiere advisors are so in tune with their clients' goals that they can actually anticipate what a client will require at different stages of their financial life. They're able to recognize important milestones and nothing falls through the cracks because they already have a system in place. Business development never gets squeezed out because their system ensures it happens every week.

Successful businesses have clearly defined repeatable systems for every important aspect of the business. These processes give you economies of scale. They allow you to reach more people and complete more tasks in less time. How you spend that extra time is completely up to you.

So, who exactly should read this book? If you'd like to grow and increase your production, it's a no-brainer. This book is for you. If you'd like to continue to do the same production but have more time to spend with friends, family and loved ones, again, a no brainer. This book is for you.

I give you some Action Steps in Chapter One to help you define goals for your practice. At the end of each chapter I will have Action Steps to help you get started with the concepts presented in the chapters.

Chances are you're good at sales. To reach your current level of production, you had to be.

Just think of the possibilities in your business and your life if you could learn to run your business like an actual business.

Regardless of whether you want to grow or just have more life balance, acquiring this specific skill set will make you look and feel more professional. You'll have the time to give your clients your very best—which makes you more referable. The more referable you are, the faster your business grows and the faster it grows, the more time you'll have to do what is important to you. You reach a point where you can even be selective about with whom you want to work.

Look at your cell phone. Chances are you work as hard as you do because you care about the people in that background picture.

Over the years, I've seen an interesting phenomenon play out with advisors on a daily basis. I have found no matter what advisors are doing, they often feel conflicted—like they should be doing something else. You have a lot of freedom in your business which sometimes can be a double-edged sword. It's one of the things that draws people to the business, but it can easily become your own worst enemy.

You've worked incredibly hard to get where you are and maybe you'd like to just start taking Fridays off in the summer. Wouldn't be nice if you could start taking that long weekend with a clear conscience? Or maybe, if you're in growth mode, wouldn't be nice to buy that new car without guilt?

What we do is a noble profession. Don't let anyone convince you otherwise. This book is about systematizing your business and giving you the tools to strategically plan for the next phase of your career—regardless of what that may look like to you. The systems I discuss ultimately hand you back control over your business.

Just like children who crave structure but constantly fight it, I understand that the idea of building systems for your business may not excite you at this point. In fact, you may even fight it. However, when you start working your business like a real business, that's when your business starts working for you.

CHAPTER 1

What Do You Want Out of Your Business?

"The only limit to our realization of tomorrow will be our doubts of today."

— Franklin D. Roosevelt

As of 2018, Cerulli and Associates, a leading industry research firm estimates that there are approximately 300,000 financial advisors in the US.[1] The average advisor is over 50 years of age and "advisors who are 55 years or older manage 36.9% of assets and comprise 39.2% of headcount."[2] The Baby Boomers are retiring at a staggering rate and 10,000 a day will turn 65 for the next twenty years and create more demand for financial advisors.[3]

These statistics point to a tremendous opportunity for advisors as we likely face a talent shortage in the coming years. The Great Recession in 2008 and precipitous market downturns in 2020 have eliminated many new advisors so established advisors, like you, are left to manage this business.

People get into this business for many different reasons. Some advisors get in because they want to make a difference in people's lives. Other people get in because they think it's sexy. They envision themselves driving fancy cars and

---

[1] Michael Kitces, "3 Reasons Why The Financial Advisor Market Sized Isn't Actually Shrinking," *Kitces Nerd's Eye View,* November 15, 2018, https://www.kitces.com/blog/financial-advisor-headcount-total-addressable-market-tam-technology-hiring-growth/

[2] "Babybust? Only 11.7% of financial advisors are under 35: Cerulli," *The Retirement Income Journal,* March 8, 2018, https://retirementincomejournal.com/article/babybust-only-11-7-of-financial-advisors-are-under-35-cerulli/

[3] Ibid.

having in-depth discussions about the markets all day long. Others get in, and this one's almost laughable, because they think of the business as a get-rich-quick occupation. Invariably, their perception of our business and the day-to-day reality of it are quite a bit different.

As a rookie, you struggle just to stay alive. After a few years, you realize you're going to make it, and this is indeed, your long-term career. You spend the next 10 years working and growing to provide a comfortable living for you and your family. You now have a legitimate business.

There's a good chance that up until this point, you've built your business around a series of default habits you've acquired over the years. You know how to work hard, people like and trust you, and you genuinely know that your clients need you. You've worked hard to get to this point, but at this stage of your career, it's important to become more strategic and refine your business to serve you and better reflect your priorities in life.

Obviously, the first priorities are to do a good job for your clients, make a comfortable living and accumulate assets for your own retirement. Most advisors don't think much past that. I'd like you to start thinking about what you want from your business beyond the obvious.

We start with your goals for your business. I'm not talking about the goals and I'm not talking about asset and revenue goals you develop as part of your business planning every year. Think in terms of big picture goals.

Your goals may encompass one or a combination of the following:

- Grow and make more money.
- Keep production constant and work less hours.
- Create a legacy. After all, there is no better estate planning tool out there than this business! I've seen some amazing parent/child teams over the years. This business gives you a fantastic tool for passing on wealth immediately to your child and teaching them about business and life at the same time. I've also seen advisors put together rock solid estate plans for

their own assets and their heirs are eternally grateful.

- Create a practice with intention.

This is our foundation. Your goals, in part, determine the systems you'll build for your business and how you will build them. This is an important first step, so plan on taking an afternoon alone outside of the office to really think this through and determine exactly what you want from your business. Remember, there is no right or wrong answer. This is all about you, written by you and for your benefit.

Client Contact

There are certain processes you simply must have in place in order to be successful and create a business model that serves you. For instance, your ability to leverage your existing book for more assets, revenue, and referrals begins and ends with your client contact system. You'd be surprised at how many advisors I come across who have no real system at all for client contact and service. Their process consists of scanning a client list for those they haven't called in a while.

I've had countless conversations with advisors and when I ask if they've talked with all of their clients in the last year, for the most part, they say, yes. When I ask how they keep track, they tell me that they just know.

This my friends, is not a system. This is a perfect example of one of those default habits you acquired along the way. It got you to this point but it will not serve you well going forward. Your client contact schedule and service model are a key foundational system in your business.

We'll go into depth on the components that should be included in your client contact system in a later chapter. For now, know that building this system begins with knowing exactly who's who in your book. You do this by working with a comprehensive book segmentation process. This includes not only consideration of assets and revenue but also certain intangibles that are essential to comprehensively segmenting your book.

Advisors always think they know their book and for the most part they do. However, whenever I take an advisor through the book segmentation process, there are always surprises and it's usually the intangibles that provide them. These include factors like:

- Do you enjoy working with them?
Have they given you referrals in the past?
- Are they an advocate?
- What kind of COI potential do they have?
- What kind of future revenue potential do you think they may have?

You may have clients you thought were A clients who turn out to be B or even C clients when you factor in the intangibles. Likewise, you may have a B or C client who moves up the food chain to a B+ or A when intangibles are considered.

For example, you may have a young couple that has tremendous potential but they don't really have a lot of assets to work with. They may be a resident doctor getting their first job or a promising young lawyer. They will eventually be wealthy but just not yet and you want to work with them now so they become a loyal fan and eventually have the assets to meet your minimums. I call them HENRYs. That's an acronym for High Earner Not Rich Yet.[4]

Once your book is segmented, then we can begin to develop a client contact schedule designed to increase your level of service, your assets under management, and your referral factor. However, the most important thing to remember when developing a client contact schedule is that it is maintainable. No matter what else is going on in the markets, in your firm, in your branch and in your life.

I see advisors fall into the overly ambitious client contact trap all the time. They start off with a killer client service plan only to discover after a couple of weeks that they can't keep up with it. There is nothing worse than showering clients with fantastic service only to have to take it away from them later.

It's far better to begin with a less aggressive plan and do it consistently. Remember,

[4] Will Henton, "High Earners, Not Rich Yet (HENRYs)," *Investopedia*, updated April 6, 2019, https://www.investopedia.com/terms/h/high-earners-not-yet-rich-henrys.asp

consistency is the sign of a great business and that's exactly what we're working to develop.

Referrals

Most advisors don't get the quality or quantity of referrals they want and expect because they've never properly conditioned their clients to even think in terms of referrals. The average client, unless they've been in sales before would have to have someone come up to them on the street and say, "I just won the lottery. Who's your financial advisor?" for them to even think in terms of referrals. The average person just doesn't give much thought to them.

You know what else doesn't work? Asking everyone you come in contact with, "Who do you know who might be interested in..." This strategy never has worked because most advisors don't do it.

Another reason it's never been effective is because it puts everyone in an awkward position. The advisor is uncomfortable, and it's awkward for the client as well, which is understandable. Think about it. You're asking the client the come up with a qualified prospect for you with no advance notice and with no clear idea of who you're even looking for in a client. This process is doomed to failure from the beginning.

The referral system I outline in a later chapter stresses referral conditioning. I'll provide you with a couple of low-key but highly effective conditioning techniques for planting the referral seed. The idea behind this system is to subtly let the client know that you want and expect referrals and then water that seed through the conditioning techniques.

Then, we add a proactive piece to the equation that gives you a tool for collecting a steady stream of potential referrals every month. As a mid-tier advisor, you're at the stage in your business where it should be growing primarily through referrals. If you can implement this new system for referrals and make it a habit, it can become a primary driver for your business growth.

Business Development

You may think at this stage of your career that business development is no longer necessary. You're getting a few referrals here and there and it's enough to keep your business functioning. Business development, regardless of your preference for methodology, is the lifeblood of your business and should be a constant throughout your career.

If there's one component of the business that's always the first to get squeezed out, it's business development. When it's time to prospect, most of us can always find something more pressing to do. Yet, this is the lifeblood of your business. Our business development program was so successful, we stopped using it.

There are three critical components to an effective business development system. First of all, we have to have a system that ensures business development is actually taking place and is consistently done each and every week. In essence, we want to build it into a regular weekly block that you schedule around just as you do appointments.

Prospecting feels different than regular client contact. In fact, it almost feels like you're using a different part of your brain when you're talking to prospects compared to clients. A key objective of our business development system is that we have a mechanism that allows you to get in the prospecting "zone" more often (on a weekly basis) and for longer periods of time.

In my experience, I've found that time-blocking activities helps create higher success. I try to schedule prospecting activities all on the same day, financial planning all on the same day, closing meetings all on the same day, etc. When you have purpose around your activity you get into your groove, you tend to have more success than going from prospecting to closing back to prospecting, then to financial planning and maybe asking for a referral if there is time. Ugh. That's hard and you don't get into your "flow."

Our second objective is that we have a system for targeting the right people in your business development efforts. To do this we'll discuss how you can mine your book for the clients you enjoy working with, who take advice, give you referrals and appreciate you. You're past the point in your career where you have to take everybody. Now is the time to be more selective and to target the type of people you enjoy working with. No matter how successful you may be, if you've built your book with people that make you cringe when you see their number pop up on caller ID, chances are your business will be somewhat less than fulfilling.

The final component of a powerful business development system is developing a highly effective drip system for moving prospects to clients in the most streamlined, effective, and unemotional manner. Most advisors find a way to endure the initial phases of prospecting. Follow-up is where advisors usually drop the ball. If a prospect doesn't become a client relatively quickly, many advisors lose interest and are onto the next prospect even when they know that person has money.

Let's face it. There are a lot of emotional ups and downs inherent in the prospecting process. A strong drip system can insulate you from much of this. When you have a good drip system, you're simply moving people through your pipeline in the most efficient manner. It becomes a matter of not if you'll land them as a client but rather when. You know how to work hard, now it's time to work smart, and creating a system to drip on your prospects to let them know you're thinking about them is important.

Branding

This business is a contact sport. It's important that you're out there getting referrals and new business all the time. Clarifying your message about what sets you apart and then communicating that message consistently and effectively is critical to your success. You must be intentional and work with it all the time—even if it is only for a few minutes a day but do it every day.

I like to use the example of, "15 minutes can save you 15% or more on car insurance." That's not exactly a catchy phrase, but we've been conditioned so well that we know exactly what company they're talking about when we hear it. We want to do the same thing for you and your business, and that's why you must have a branding system in place.

Branding is dependent on conditioning and conditioning is purely a function of repetition. What do you say when someone asks you what you do for a living? If your reply is that you're a financial advisor with XYZ, then you've just blown a golden opportunity to hook a prospect and capture their attention.

To be effective, there are several components a good branding system must have, and we'll talk about each of those later in the book. We want to train your clients to be saying the right things about you when your name comes up in public. Your branding statement basically encapsulates your reputation. This is what you want people to most remember about you and be able to easily communicate to others. This is far too important to leave to chance, which is precisely why you must have a system for it and apply that system consistently and universally.

Here's an example that illustrates the power of branding. My wife works in the emergency room. Over her scrubs, she wears a white lab coat with a stethoscope draped over her neck. One morning, before her shift, she was running around the house looking in all the drawers. I asked her what she was looking for and she said, "clicky pens." The type that you need to click versus one with a cap. I asked why "clicky pens" and she said because the other types leave a black or a blue mark when she slides it into her chest pocket.

The pharmaceutical companies were not allowed to come to the ER and leave their pens so she needed pens. I decided that I would buy "clicky pens" with my name, company and toll-free number on them and every time I dropped by, I would leave some pens behind. They were a HUGE hit. I also left them in my suit pockets so many times that almost all the pens at the dry cleaners were my pens! I also left them with waiters and waitresses when I went out to eat!

The reason I tell you this story is not because someone saw my pens and called me to invest a million dollars. That never happened. However, the people I came in contact with said that they saw my pens! The ER staff knew that I was the money guy. For years, people would ask me financial questions because they were comfortable with me and they trusted me...and it all started with "clicky pens."

Time Management

Finally, you must have some sort of system for managing your time. You're in a highly reactive business and it can be challenging to develop a proactive approach to your time. Generally speaking, advisors spend way too much time trying to decide what to do next. Couple that with a constant stream of interruptions throughout your day and you can easily lose two hours a day just trying to get back on task after being interrupted.

Another advisor habit I've observed over the years concerns how you're actually spending your time. What advisors think they're doing and what they're actually doing are often two completely different things. Every good time management system should include a tracking component precisely for this reason. It doesn't really matter what you use, as long as you use something that you like and will use.

Time management systems are highly individualized and can be as structured or as loose as need be, depending on what works for you. I've tried just about every time management system available. I finally stumbled upon one that advisors have found highly effective.

It's very different than anything you've probably ever used so it will take some adjustment. If you have a time management system that works for you, by all means keep it, but at least scan the system I lay out later in the book. What I hear from every advisor who's implemented it is, it's like adding hours to your day and no one day every seems overwhelming anymore. You get a lot more done in lot less time.

It's never too early or too late to start building systems for your business. Eventually, you will reach a point in your career when you've outgrown the old piecemeal approach to your business model. Remember, what got you here may not get you there. Systems help you to reach your goals faster, easier and with less stress regardless of whether your goal is to grow, raise the level of service you provide to clients, have more free time or some combination of these.

EMOTIONAL VICTORIES SYSTEMATIC FAILURES

In the first part of your career, the focus was on surviving. In this next phase of your career, the focus is on thriving and building a business that suits your personality. To do this, we'll build systems around you, your priorities and the lifestyle you desire. You know how to work hard, now it is time to work *smart*.

Chapter 1 Action Steps

Chapter 1 is a great place to start gaining clarity. Begin by asking yourself these questions and be honest with yourself.

- Why did you get into this business?
- What did you do to be successful?
- What motivates you now?
- Why do you stay in this business?
- Where do you want to go?

www.eliasrdau.com
me@eliasrdau.com

CHAPTER 2

Survivors: The Nature of the Advisor Personality

"By choosing our path, we choose our destination."

— Anonymous

Financial advisors are survivors by nature. Think about it. You're hit with adversity virtually every single day as you navigate markets, money, clients, prospects, politics, world events—and even pandemics. You *have* to be a survivor.

ELIAS R. DAU, CRPC®

Most people dealing with these kinds of circumstances on a daily basis may shut down or feel like a victim. Some may feel helpless or overwhelmed. They may even find themselves blaming others around them for their difficulties.

Not so with successful financial advisors. You find a way to build strength through adversity and have a knack for turning problems or apparent misfortunes into opportunity. Successful advisors find ways to thrive through crisis. You recover quickly, adapt well, and have found ways to cope with the constant pressure and change inherent in the business.

Over the years, I've discovered that most people seldom access their greatest strengths and abilities until forced to do so by a challenge or crisis. Julius Segal, a world-renown researcher on the survivor personality commented, "In a remarkable number of cases, those who have suffered and prevail find that after their ordeal they begin to operate at a higher level than ever before. . . The terrible experiences of our lives, despite the pain they bring, may become our redemption."[5]

The advisors who thrive do so because they choose to perceive their difficulties as opportunities for personal growth. They are resilient and resilience is nothing more than a measure of your ability to go with the flow and roll with whatever life throws at you. Successful advisors believe in themselves and the value they bring to clients. It's that belief in their ability to make a positive impact on their clients' lives that keep them going in the face of problems, challenges, and rejection. When faced with adversity, they overcome and continue to move forward.

Resilience

Resilience is what keeps you going as you overcome obstacles on your way to achieving your goals. It's a test of your inner strength and it's what pushes you through difficult problems and challenges.

---

[5] Al Siebert, "The Survivor Personality Chapter 1," *Practical Psychology Press,* Accessed April 18, 2020, https://practicalpsychologypress.com/resources/survivor-personality-chapter-one/

In his book, *Unheavenly City*, Harvard University sociologist, Dr. Edward Banfield set out to discover why some people were financially successful while others were never able to achieve true financial independence. He fully expected factors such as intelligence, education, and background to be the key variables at work. However, what he discovered was that the most successful people he studied had one thing in common: the ability to maintain a long-term perspective regardless of what was going on around them. In fact, he found that the "future" was an important component of every decision they made in the present.

Nothing illustrates this better than when Hurricane Sandy hit the Northeast. We had no power and sometimes, no clean water for a week to 10 days at a time. Some advisors felt the impact immediately as they returned to find their homes a complete loss.

In my own home, I cranked up the generator and made sure most things were up and running. We filled every gas can we could find to keep the generator running. With young children, a top priority of mine was to keep that refrigerator running.

Once I had my family as settled as possible, I did what any good leader would do. I started calling my advisors to make sure they were okay. One of the first advisors I reached out to was a higher-level producer we'll call "Jake."

When he answered his cell phone, I noticed a lot of background noise but Jake let me know he was okay. When I asked him if he had been calling clients, he said yes. He'd been calling them from his cell phone and pulling up basic information on his iPad. He gave them account balances and said his clients were most concerned with how much cash they had on hand for emergency purposes. Jake added that when he needed to place a trade, he'd been calling the trading desks directly.

He apologized for the background noise and said he was in the Lowe's parking lot waiting for new generators to arrive. He planned to power up his house so he could log into the company's system. I remember telling him that wasn't going to work because his desktop computer at the office didn't have power and we remotely logged into those computers.

He laughed and said he'd called a colleague in Florida and they had a spare desktop he could connect to remotely. He was also buying a generator for his assistant and asked me if I needed one. I thanked him and told him I was fine. I can still remember saying to him, "Jake, if you were stranded on a deserted island, you'd be eating filet mignon!"

Jake personified resilience. He took a difficult situation and turned it into an opportunity to provide value to his clients. He *believed* he played an important role in their lives and his actions backed that belief up. Jake was there for his clients when they needed him the most and his clients will remember that for years to come. He used Hurricane Sandy to build the trust his clients had him. He'd always been a top producer and his survivor mentality will keep him a top producer throughout his career.

After roughly ten days, advisors started trickling back to the office. My lowest producer eventually walked in. We'll call him "Dave." I told him that I'd been trying to reach him. He quickly responded that his cell phone had died. I asked him if he'd been able to reach any of his clients. He reminded me that his cell phone had died, and he hadn't been able to contact any clients over the last 10 days.

Top producers know how to overcome obstacles. Regardless of circumstances, they never blame others. They figure out a way to not only get through the situation but shine in the eyes of clients and colleagues. Marginal producers never learn this skill or simply choose not to implement it in their career.

Positive Failure

There's an old Japanese proverb credited to Nana Korobi Ya Oki, which translates to "Fall down seven times, get up eight."[6] It speaks to the Japanese "resilience" mentality and the belief that you must get up again regardless of how many times you get knocked down. And,

---

[6] "Fall Down 7 Times, Get Up 8," *Mental Toughness Partners,* September 2, 2018, https://www.mentaltoughnesspartners.com/fall-down-seven-times-get-up-eight/

there will be many of these instances throughout your career.

When plans don't work out, your default response may be to think you have failed. However, it's far more beneficial to your psyche and your career to force a paradigm shift in your own mind. Begin to think of failure as nothing more than extremely valuable feedback. When you view a situation as a failure, chances are that you'll give up more easily and your confidence erodes. Failure has negative connotations. It's a dead end.

Feedback, on the other hand, is positive. It allows you to learn from past mistakes and puts you on a path to taking the corrective actions necessary to reach your goals. When you're able to change your mindset and begin thinking that there is no such thing as failure, only feedback, a funny thing happens. Eventually, you'll find yourself "failing" less and less.

When you can view failure as nothing more than feedback, you're less stressed and more motivated to persevere through whatever you must to reach your goals. Use perceived failure as a vehicle for strategic improvement. Consider failure a *constructive* critic of what you're doing and how you're doing it.

I tell my advisors all the time, **"Experience your victories emotionally and approach failures from a purely analytical basis."** Enjoy your successes. Celebrate them and feel them on an emotional level. This is how you imprint them into your subconscious. All too often, advisors don't take time to enjoy a success but rather, move immediately on to the next goal. You've worked hard for them so enjoy them.

Debrief after failures. Study them analytically. Why did they happen? What could you have done differently? How can you best be prepared for this situation when it happens again? What did you learn about your process and yourself? These are all questions you should ask yourself every time things don't go as planned.

Approaching failures from an analytical perspective diffuses a lot of the emotion associated with the failure. In addition to viewing the situation more objectively, it also helps you to move through negative circumstances far more quickly.

It's also important that we each own our mistakes and learn from them. There really is no such thing as a mistake if you're able to learn from it. Our intentions are always in the right place when helping our clients but mistakes are inevitable. Sometimes the mistake is ours, other times it may belong to another team member and sometimes it's a firm mistake. Unfortunately, this is a fact of life. #$&! happens, right? Regardless of whether the mistake is large or small, if you're anything like me, it makes you want to crawl under a rock and hide for a while.

One of my big mistakes happened about ten years ago. A client was buying a property and we needed to raise some cash, so we sold some investments. We would issue a certified check that they could bring to closing on Tuesday and the transaction would close on time. One small problem...I forgot that Monday was a bank holiday so the funds would take an extra day to settle. To make a long story short, the funds would not be available in time and the client would have to delay the closing an extra day. It doesn't seem like a big issue but the seller wanted to close on Tuesday so we had to figure it out. After a couple hours of phone calls and emails, my firm was able to front the cash for the certified check and they were able to close on their transaction the same day. It was a horrible experience for the client, my team, my manager, and me.

The very first thing I did was to own my mistake. I told them that it was my fault and that I would do everything I could to make it right. I walked them through the different courses of action we were taking but there was still a chance they may not receive their check until the following day. I reassured them throughout the day that we were doing everything we could to make it right.

I wanted to make it up to the client so I ordered some steaks (under $100) online for them and in my note, I apologized for the mishap and hoped they would accept my "Steaks for Mistakes." A few days later, the clients received the gift and they were elated. I even added a little dessert! I received the call from them immediately letting me know that they wished I made those mistakes more often!

The moral of the story is that we need to own the mistakes, whether we made them or not. Acknowledge the mistake, and apologize. Alexander Pope said, "To err is human; to forgive, is divine."[7]

Recovering from Setbacks

Failure is inevitable. If you've never failed at something before, chances are you've never tried anything challenging before. And, if you have failed in the past, it does *not* mean that you are a failure. Part of using failure as feedback and a positive in your life involves being able to recover from it quickly and use the lessons learned to adjust your strategy going forward.

One thing I always say to advisors I'm coaching goes something like this, "When a high performing advisor sees an obstacle, they don't blame other people for the obstacle being in the way. They don't blame their manager, the markets, legislation, interest rates, or anything

[7] "Alexander Pope Quotes," *Brain Quote*, Accessed August 1, 2020,
https://www.brainyquote.com/quotes/alexander_pope_101451

else. The good advisors, the really great ones, find a way to get over, under, around, or through that obstacle."

After working with advisors for many years, I've identified five key actions that can help you to recover from setbacks quicker and use feedback information more effectively to make appropriate adjustments.

Reaffirm

Successful advisors constantly visualize their desired outcome and reaffirm to themselves that their goals are credible and achievable. Don't for a minute think that successful advisors never entertain negative feelings. They do. The difference is they use the power of their mind to stop those thoughts in their tracks. Whenever thoughts of "I can't do it," enter their mind, they consciously replace them with thoughts of, "Yes I can."

By using this simple strategy on a consistent basis, you can actually influence your subconscious mind. By remolding your thoughts and attitude, you're able to transform your behavior. When your behavior changes, your life changes.

Forgive

Forgiving yourself and learning from your mistakes can be a key success driver in your life. Successful advisors don't beat themselves for long after they make a mistake. They recognize that being hypercritical depletes confidence, making it more difficult to rebound after a perceived setback.

Reflect

Learning opportunities emerge from both success and failure. They say you learn much more from your perceived failures than you do from your successes. Reflecting on failures gives you clarity on both your strengths and weaknesses. You begin to identify your own personal blind spots, insecurities, and quirks. When you're able to reflect on failures analytically and objectively, you can make informed adjustments and plot a more effective course of action in future.

Manage

Your ability to manage self-doubt and reframe negative self-talk is one of the most important skills you must master. It is absolutely critical to your long-term success. When successful advisors make mistakes or experience setbacks, they analyze their feelings objectively. They develop strategies and strong mental arguments to battle their negative self-talk and doubt.

I've known advisors who succinctly write down in detail their thoughts, fears, doubts, and concerns surrounding a setback or failure. They then challenge them with rational thoughts and arguments. Often, their worries and doubts disappear as a result of this process. However, if their concerns are legitimate and entail genuine risk, they create a new plan and take additional measures to produce their desired outcome.

This process is a confidence-boosting one and makes even the worst of problems seem doable. Henry Ford said, "Whether you think you can or whether you think you can't, you're right."[8] Success always begins in your mind. Successful advisors know this and tweak this approach to fit them and base new processes and systems on what they've learned in the past.

Thomas Edison, one of this country's most well-known inventors learned to embrace failure. This led to his relentless persistence in creating new ways to achieve his goals. His famous quote on the subject is, "I have not failed; I have just found 10,000 ways that won't work."[9] Just think about what an amazing impact an attitude like that could have on your business. Take it from Tom!

Recommit

Successful advisors don't stay down. They recalibrate, get back on their feet and recommit

---

[8] Jennifer Foster, "Whether You Think You Can Or Whether You Think You Can't, You're Right," *Wall Street Insanity,* Accessed April 19, 2020, https://wallstreetinsanity.com/whether-you-think-you-can-or-whether-you-think-you-cant-youre-right/

[9] "I Have not Failed. I've Just 10,000 Ways It Won't Work," *Mr. Great Motivation,* Accessed August 1, 2020, https://www.mrgreatmotivation.com/2017/12/i-have-not-failed-i-have-just-found.html

to their success. They may begin a little more cautiously after a major setback, but they begin. Proactive, productive activity builds confidence. Starting and making small, incremental but intentional steps armed with your lessons from the past cultivates strong self-belief. Every step you take after a perceived failure is proof of your resolve. Every success is a testament to your commitment.

Jim Rohn once said, "Success is not to be pursued. It is to be attracted by the person you become."[10] To achieve a new level of success, you will change and become a new person along the way. Visualize the success you desire. Now, what does a day in the life of your future self look like?

Spend some time thinking about that. What are you doing? How is your thinking different? Do you act differently? Where are you living? What are you feeling? What does your

---

[10] "20 Inspirational Quotes From Jim Rohn," *Habits for Well-Being,* Accessed April 19, 2020, https://www.habitsforwellbeing.com/20-inspirational-quotes-from-jim-rohn/

environment look like? How are you perceived by your family, friends, and colleagues?

We all have some vision of what success would look like to us. Start taking steps today to become your future successful self. Start thinking like you would if you had achieved all your goals. Act like the success you envision.

Success begins in your head. Allow your mind to focus on what you want and keep your thoughts away from everything you don't. It's very easy to let an undisciplined mind linger on negativity and unproductive self-talk. The ability to transmute your negative thoughts into positive ones is one of the most important skills an advisor can acquire.

When you can do this, you can build confidence and resilience. Reframe failures and setbacks as learning experiences because remember, there is no failure, only feedback. This is a fantastic business. It gives you tremendous freedom and virtually unlimited revenue potential. You are a survivor by your very nature. Now it's time to become a thriver.

There's a very famous story of two lumberjacks that I've heard for many years in the business that I'd like to share with you. One of the lumberjacks had years of experience while the other one was young and inexperienced but sported a healthy ego. One day, the younger man challenged the experienced lumberjack to a contest to see who could chop down the most tress in a day.

The young lumberjack started chopping immediately and didn't stop all day. He knew he had this contest in the bag. There was no way the old guy was going to beat him—especially since he took a 15-minute break every hour.

At the end of the day, much to the younger man's astonishment, the older, experienced lumberjack had cut down 25% more trees. Swallowing his pride, the young man asked the victor how he could possibly have beat him when he took a 15-minute break every hour.

He smiled and answered that he took a 15-minute break every hour to sharpen his ax. This was his secret to success.

Successful advisors always find the time to plan, read, research, exercise and eat healthy foods. This is equivalent to sharpening your ax in our business. Take your growth seriously, plan for it strategically and, never stop sharpening your ax.

Chapter 2 Action Steps

Think of a failure in your past and answer the questions below:

- How did it make you feel?
- How did you react?
- What circumstances were out of your control?
- What was in your control?
- How do you see that situation from your perspective now?
- What did you learn?
- How have you modified your behavior since then?

www.eliasrdau.com
me@eliasrdau.com

• C H A P T E R 3 •

Why Volatility is Your Friend

"The way I see it, if you want the rainbow, you gotta put up with the rain."

— Dolly Parton

As I write this chapter, we are in the middle of the Coronavirus pandemic. The country is still shut down and only businesses deemed essential by the state are allowed to operate. The curve may be starting to flatten. However, as we move closer to reopening the country, there is much debate on when and how the government should proceed.

We are living in unprecedented times. Most people have been out of work and quarantined at home for months. Grocery store shelves are sparse. Schools have been closed since Spring and many may not even open in the fall with students beginning their school year virtually. The class of 2020 was born the same year that 9/11 happened and they will graduate at home, in solitude, away from their friends. On the news tonight I watched as cars lined up at the Pittsburgh airport and waited hours to get food.

On March 16, 2020 the CBOE Volatility Index, known as the VIX closed at a record high of 82.69. This surpassed its previous high of 80.74 on November 21, 2008.[11] Over the last eight weeks, it's not unusual to see the Dow fluctuate by 300-500 points a day. What a great time to write a chapter on volatility!

---

[11] Yun Li, "Wall Street's Fear Gauge Closes At Its Highest Level Ever, Surpassing Even Financial Crisis Peak," *CNBC,* March 16, 2020, https://www.cnbc.com/2020/03/16/wall-streets-fear-gauge-hits-highest-level-ever.html

Advisors who weren't in this business in 2008 and have never experienced a down market have found this recent volatility particularly disturbing. There have been many crises in recent years that precipitated a down market laced with volatility: the stock market crash of 1987; the tech bubble of 2000; the financial crisis in 2008; and now the pandemic of 2020. It's very tempting to think each time that this time is different. What if this is the time when markets don't recover?

Since 1926, there have been 16 bear markets. They've lasted an average of 22 months and pushed the market down an average of 39%.[12] However, the stock market still has had more up days than down days. From 1950 through 2019, the S&P 500 closed up 53.7% of the time and down 46.3% of the time, with positive days exceeding negative days in every decade.[13]

The circumstances that lead to extreme volatility and down markets are always different

---

[12] Dana Anspach, "U.S. Stock Bear Markets And Their Subsequent Recoveries," *The Balance,* March 20, 2020, https://www.thebalance.com/u-s-stock-bear-markets-and-their-subsequent-recoveries-2388520
[13] Ibid

but how the markets behave is always the same. Let me reiterate this point. **The reason or reasons a market has a precipitous decline will be different almost every time, but the months and years that follow reward the investors that stayed true to their course.** Bull markets usually follow bear markets and often last for years. A substantial portion of bull market gains usually occur during the early months of an upturn. According to a recent report from Fidelity, since 1929, in the year following the bottom of a bear market, the S&P 500 has averaged a whopping 47% gain.[14]

With volatility comes uncertainty. It also brings tremendous opportunity for both clients and advisors. This is when advisors earn their keep. No matter how much you try to prepare clients, volatility always seems to catch them by surprise. It stirs that primal emotion: fear.

A critical part of your job as an advisor is to manage client fears. You do that by being engaged, empathetic and stepping up communication to clients during difficult

---

[14] Ibid.

markets. Your primary objective with each market downturn should be to go above and beyond in terms of client contact, build trust and increase your "referability" factor.

Instead of becoming apprehensive about volatility, consider it your friend. Think about it for a minute. When markets go straight up, clients and prospects don't see your value. When they go straight down, they question your value. However, when volatility runs rampant, clients and prospects want to talk to you. They want you to tell them what to do. Recognize this as a golden opportunity and take advantage it.

I've been an advisor through the tech bubble, 2008 and now 2020 and one rule that I have followed is this. When the VIX is above 20, I proactively call my clients. I call them on a frequent basis to check in. In 2008, I developed this strategy. I moved most of my practice to fee-based relationships in 2007 and by March of 2008, the markets were tumbling. I knew that if I didn't call my clients, someone else would, and in those unprecedented times, who knows what they would do and where they would go.

Another advisor once told me that when the VIX hits 20, that it is a technical indicator of a market drop. I don't follow technical analysis but I did find it alarming, so I started calling clients to check in on them.

The initial calls were difficult, but I reassured them that the strategy we had in place was the right one for them. If we needed to rebalance or make a minor "course correction" then we would make those changes.

The tone of the calls changed when large financial institutions were falling. This was the second phase of the 2008 collapse. Clients started asking about FDIC and SIPC insurance. I learned more about those programs and reinsurance by Lloyd's of London than I would ever care to know.

The third phase was a bit unexpected. I started receiving more money from my clients. They had assets held away and were not satisfied with their relationship. Rates and returns were down for everyone and once they understood it, they began to value our relationship more. It wasn't long before they began bringing additional assets over. They even started to refer the people they cared about. They finally understood how much I cared about them and remembered that I was there for them through the darkest of days.

The final phase was the most profound for me. I had been calling almost all my clients weekly for several months and by the Fall, the tone of these conversations changed again. Clients started asking how I was doing. They were concerned about me and my family.

At that point, I knew that my relationship with my clients had just evolved into a more meaningful relationship. This changed my career and I developed a true appreciation for why I was doing what I was doing.

Use Volatility to Build and Deepen Relationships

When markets are volatile, this is your chance to reinforce to clients and prospects your value and what an integral part you play in helping them reach their financial goals. Over the years, I've seen successful advisors utilize declining markets very effectively to build trust and deepen relationships. Here are five tips for doing so:

1. **Know what your core message is and be able to clearly articulate it.** What is it you most want clients to know during difficult times? Is it that you're monitoring things closely and now is the time to put some cash to work? Or is it that you understand that market volatility can be worrisome and you're there for them? Regardless of what your message may be, you must communicate this to clients and prospects often and consistently. If you sell performance, you will get fired for performance. If you have a strategy and they buy into the strategy, you're far less likely to get fired by your client in a market downturn.

2. **Overcommunicate.** When it comes right down to it, all clients really want to know is that you're watching the markets, you're on top of things, and that you're looking out for them. Put the client first

and use every opportunity to reiterate this to them. When markets are volatile, emotions run high. Be a good listener. Sometimes that's all a client needs.

3. **Never underestimate the power of a soft touch.** I have found that advisors who are able to master the art of soft touches tend to be far more successful than those who don't. A good soft touch is a powerful business-building tool. In addition to making the client feel good, it has the potential to generate the unsolicited positive word-of-mouth exposure that money can't buy.

    One of my favorite examples of a successful soft touch was an advisor in my office had a client whose dogs were like her children. When he called her, he discovered that one of her dogs had to have surgery and she was distraught over it. He sent the dog a get-well card addressed to the dog. That client told everyone she knew about it and he ended up with two referrals from a card that cost him a couple of bucks.

Soft touches tell the client that you're attentive and interested in them. They also show your human side and establish you as a warm and caring person. Never underestimate the power of the soft touch, especially in volatile times.

4. **Encourage referrals.** Advisors are usually pretty good at reaching out to clients when a market downturn first occurs. However, the longer it goes on, the more client contact starts to drop off. Advisors often are hesitant to call clients who are losing money. Sometimes, they don't know what to do so they do nothing. Notice I said encourage referrals—I didn't say ask for referrals. Remember, when markets are volatile, clients and prospects want to hear what you have to say. Use this opportunity to plant a referral seed. Let them know that if they have friends or family members who aren't getting the

kind of service they want and need during these volatile times you'd be glad to help them out any way you can. Not only does this let them know in a non-threatening manner that you want referrals, it also reinforces that they are getting the kind of service they want and need.

5. **Volatility loves company.** Bring your clients together like family. Assuming social distancing is a temporary aberration, this gives clients a chance to discuss what's going on in casual atmosphere. It also serves as one of those powerful soft touches.

How to Keep & Gain Clients in Market Downturns

As you well know, there are many aspects of the business over which you have no control — the markets, interest rates, politics, legislation, and company policy to name a few. This is why it's so important to your sanity and success that you stay focused on the components of the business you can control.

No matter what's going on in the markets or around the world, you will always have control over your attitude, your effort, and your activity. When I talk about activity, I'm talking about proactive, productive activity—the kind that produces results. Do the things that matter most first.

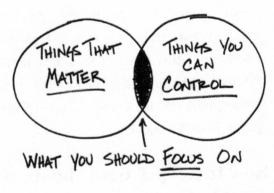

https://behaviorgap.com/

Communication

We've already established how important communication is during volatile times. It's important that clients and prospects hear significant market news from you first and not on CNBC. This can be a challenge for advisors who have a lot of households.

One of the best ways to manage client contact during volatile times is to do a communication segmentation of your book. What you're doing is segmenting your book by communication priority. Segment as follows:

- Nervous Nellies
- Retirees
- Clients and prospects who plan to retire in the next 1-5 years
- Clients and prospect who could put money to work when the markets are down

Superimpose this segmentation over your regular book segmentation. In other words, work through each of the above groups first in the A tier of your book, followed by the Bs and Cs. This gives you a methodical, prioritized structure for a heavy communication load during volatile markets.

Service

It always shocks me how many advisors have no structured client service schedule and let me be perfectly clear. Scanning a spreadsheet of your clients, deciding who you haven't talked to in a while is *not* a client service schedule.

We've already established how important communication is when markets are volatile. Service and communication are the two most powerful tools you have to build your business. And, they are both components of the business that you have complete control over.

When developing a client service schedule, the most important factor to consider is how maintainable it is. I much rather see an advisor be less aggressive in terms of contact but consistent. You must be able to maintain your service schedule regardless of what's going on in the markets, the world, your life, your firm, or your office. There's nothing worse than providing clients with a killer service schedule for a month and have to take it away because you discover you can't maintain it.

Your service schedule should include touches by your assistant, phone calls, email, events, lunches, dinners, and "surprise-and-delight" soft touches. (I'll discuss further what goes into an effective service schedule in Chapter 6.)

If you take the time to create a structured communication and service schedule, your business will grow in good times and in bad. **Your ability to leverage your existing book for more assets, revenue and referrals begins and ends with your client service/communication schedule.**

Taking Care of Yourself

This is a high-stress business. To be successful, you must take care of yourself—mentally, physically, and emotionally. How many times have you gone through an entire day without taking any time for yourself at all? And if you're like most Americans, healthy eating and regular exercise are the first things to get squeezed out of your busy schedule.

We all know what they say every time we get on a plane. If the oxygen masks drop, put it on yourself first. That way, you can help the others around you. This is a great analogy for the rest of life. If you can't take care of yourself, you can't take care of others.

Maintaining mental and physical health may seem like a huge commitment but there are small lifestyle changes you can make that will go a long way in promoting your good health. Evaluating when and where changes should be made in support of your mental and physical health is a great first step.

Mental Wellness

Every advisor is different and will feel differently about different mental wellness activities. Fortunately, there are several from which to choose. Find what resonates most with you.

One way to start with improving mental health is to engage in mental wellness activities that have been proven to boost health, wellness, and inner peace.

Each person is different and will feel differently about different types of mental wellness activities. Here are some ideas to get you started:

- **Meditation**

  There are many health benefits as well as business benefits associated with meditation. It's been found to reduce stress and increase focus in addition to improving self-esteem and reducing stress. Visualization is a form of meditation and its benefits are widely recognized in both business and professional sports.

- **Daily-Affirmation**

  Have a daily routine where you are alone and in a quiet space. Most people prefer quiet mornings. Take a deep breath, hold it and slowly release it. Do this 3-5 times. Look at yourself in the mirror and say a positive affirmation to yourself slowly and with purpose. Repeat the affirmation a few times and move on through your day.

- **Physical Activity**

  It's no secret that physical activity and exercise can significantly improve mental health. It can also help in the management of depression, anxiety and panic disorders.

- **Spend Time Outside**

  It can be difficult at times finding inner peace amidst work, family, cooking, cleaning, appointments, etc. Get away from the daily grind and spend some time in nature. Fresh air can help reduce anxiety and promote feelings of peace and balance—all of which reduce stress.

- **Socialize**

  Socializing is a great way to meet new people and build a social support network. It promotes self-efficacy, life satisfaction, and a sense of belonging. It's also great for prospecting, which is always less objectionable when you mix it with something you enjoy doing.

- **Volunteer**

  Volunteering has always been a powerful mental wellness activity because you feel like you're part of something bigger than yourself. There's no denying it—you just feel good when you offer service. It boosts self-esteem and increases feelings of self-satisfaction. It can also be a great way to meet wealthy people.

Physical Wellness

Taking care of your physical body is just as important as caring for your mental health. Taking care of yourself physically doesn't necessarily mean long grueling hours at the gym. There are many small things you can do that can make a big difference in your physical health.

The following activities help promote a healthy body:

- **Drink More Water**
  Your body is predominantly water and needs it to function. For your body to function at optimum levels, you must stay hydrated. Simply drinking more water can improve energy levels and flush out toxins. Keep that water bottle handy!
- **Get More Sleep**
  Sleep gives your body a chance to heal and recharge. It's always a good idea to eliminate screen time before bed as well as stimulants such as caffeine and alcohol. Get a good night's sleep to have more energy the next day.
- **Have Good Work-Life Balance**
  Work has a tendency to monopolize large chunks of time. If work is consuming all your time and energy, it might be a good idea to evaluate how you're using your time. Maintaining a solid work-life balance increases life satisfaction while reducing stress levels.

- **Relax**

  Relaxation is a personal thing. Do what works for you. Taking a few minutes out of your day to focus on whatever you find relaxing is great for the mind and keeps your stress levels low.

- **Eat Better**

  Easting healthy can be a challenge. Start wherever you are and commit to making one healthy change for the next week. Strive for consistency. Beware of convenient pre-packaged foods. They often sacrifice nutritional value for convenience.

It's important that you take the time to take care of your mental and physical health so you can always be at your best for clients, prospects, friends, and family. Focus on the components of the business you can control and always remember that volatility is your friend. It gives you wonderful opportunities to build deeper relationships with prospects and clients. Leverage volatility to your advantage. It's in volatile times like these that advisors earn their keep.

ELIAS R. DAU, CRPC®

Chapter 3 Action Steps

1. Create a communication plan for times of volatility. Know what method of communication your clients prefer: Calls, email, social media, text, or face to face.
Do they prefer facts and figures? Charts? Quotes? Stories?

2. If the VIX goes over 20, you know what to do! Call your clients!!!

3. time for yourself every day. In a high-stress business like ours, the is *not* optional.

4. Create a daily ritual that will help you be a better person and allow you to help others more.

www.eliasrdau.com
me@eliasrdau.com

•   C H A P T E R   4   •

Have a Process and a Plan

"Plan for what is difficult while it is easy, do what is great while it is small."

— Sun Tzu

There comes a time in your career when you have to take a step back from working *in* your business to work *on* your business if you hope to reach the next level. Where this exact point lies in your career depends on the nature of your business. For some advisors this point may be before they even hit $100,000 in production. For others it may be closer to $300,000 and for others, it could be $500,000. The truth is you can only "fly by the seat of your pants" for so long. Sooner or later the infrastructure of your business must be addressed if you are to reach your full potential as an advisor.

To gain the power of leverage over your time and your book, you must have clearly defined, repeatable systems in place for the key aspects of your business. Systems are good for the client because your level of service increases as a result of having them in place. They can also save you time. Your business operates more efficiently and you look and feel more professional.

After many years in the business, I've identified nine specific areas where having a repeatable process in place can help you to grow much faster and more efficiently. Your ability to leverage your existing book for more assets, revenue and referrals is largely dependent on the systems you have in place.

Time Management

Morning Ritual: This doesn't have to be long. What can you do in 15-20 minutes every morning that will set yourself up for success each day? For some that could be going to the gym. For others, it may be reading or meditating. Decide what actions would work for you and commit to them. Rushing out of the door stressed before the day even begins and to a drive-thru for breakfast is not exactly a "breakfast of champions."

To-Do List: A daily to-do list is non-negotiable. Yet, you'd be shocked at how many advisors walk into the office cold — with absolutely no idea of what they're going to do for the day. Every day, I see advisors waste an incredible amount of time trying to figure out what to do next. Create your to-do list before you leave the office for the next day or as part of your morning ritual. **Do not wait until you get to the office to do it!** Having your to-do list in hand upon arriving at the office helps you to get right back on task with minimum downtime, regardless of what's going on in the markets, with clients or in the office.

Time-Block by Day Not by Hours: Let's face it — in general, Mondays and Fridays typically aren't the most productive days for advisors. Mondays are basically a weekend-recovery day. No one really likes to make calls or receive calls on Mondays. Most people are just trying to prime themselves for the upcoming week.

The same is true on Fridays. Everyone is working for the weekend and by Friday most energy is consumed with plans for the weekend. You want to set yourself up to make every day of the week a productive day. Over the years, I've tried virtually every time management system out there and although, time-blocking by day may feel odd at first, it allows you to get in the "zone" more often and for longer periods of time. Here's how it works.

Everything non-call related is done on Monday. This includes all your call and appointment prep work, proposals, research and planning for the week. Make a list of who you intend to call for the week and what you're going to talk to them about. Anything that will better prepare you for the rest of the week and allow you to move from task to task seamlessly – do on Mondays.

Fridays are your clean-up day. It's your opportunity to take care of everything that didn't get done for the week. Begin to rough out your Monday agenda on Fridays. Tuesdays and Thursdays are client days. Do everything client-related on Tuesdays and Thursdays: your calls, appointments, lunches, and events. Try to leave Fridays open so you can catch up on anything you missed during the week. Talk to clients who may have questions, finish conversations and tie up loose ends so Friday can be dedicated to positive conversations. It's great to finish the week on a positive note.

Wednesdays are your business development day. Business development is always the first thing to get squeezed out when you're busy. Having a dedicated business development day ensures that you're doing some business development work each week.

I don't know about you, but I never call a client on a Monday and ask them for a decision.

Your closing ratio is probably pretty dismal compared to any other day of the work week.

The primary aim of this strategy is to land you in your productive "zone" more often and for longer periods of time. You're also utilizing more of your week for productive activity.

Organization

Learn to Love Checklists: They are your friend. Get in the habit of using checklists for everything and I don't mean on sticky notes. If you are a techie, there are many apps you can use. I like one called *Checklist+*. Another option is to get a 5-subject notebook. Create 5 broad list categories and add your checklists in the appropriate section.

If you think checklists aren't necessary, think again. Doctors use them every day in the operating room and pilots have lengthy checklists they must follow before taking off. Checklists minimize the possibility of tasks falling through the cracks which makes you look and feel more professional.

In 2009, the *New England Journal of Medicine* published an article about the effectiveness of using checklists in the operating room. In the study, they found that surgical teams who utilized a simple checklist saw patient mortality rates cut nearly in half and complications decreased by more than a third.[15]

Dr. Atul Gawande, an associate professor at Harvard School of Public Health shared one story of a surgery where he was to remove an adrenal tumor. The anesthesiologist who was using a checklist at the time noticed that the patient might require extra blood that was not currently on hand. They ordered the extra blood which the patient did end up needing.

"I'm convinced that the fact that the anesthesiologist caught that was what saved this man's life," Gawande says, adding that his team avoids at least one potential problem via the checklist every week.[16]

---

[15] Maia Szalavitz, "Study: A Simple Surgery Checklist Saves Lives," *Time,* January 14, 2009, http://content.time.com/time/health/article/0,8599,1871759,00.html

[16] Ibid.

When surgical teams started to use checklists, they helped to save thousands of lives. If checklists can make that dramatic difference in the operating room, just imagine the impact they can have in your business if you use them strategically and consistently.

Leverage Technology: Firms roll out new technology on an almost daily basis. (Technology Update Mondays are the bane of my existence) Develop the habit of staying on top of your firm's tech resources, or at least have someone on your team who can show you how these updates can help you. Yes, this does require a certain investment of time. However, the time saved and the increase in effectiveness usually far outweigh the time invested. Whenever you're able to do one or both, you're essentially creating capacity in your business.

These days, social media has taken on a more prominent role than ever before in nearly every advisor's business. This is another area where leveraging technology can save you a ton of time. Automate as many phases of your social media presence as you possibly can. With as much time as we spend on social media every day, even small changes can add up to large chunks of time saved. For instance, even something as simple as scheduling your posts ahead of time for the month or week can free up more time than you think. More and more, firms are offering various services to help you automate different facets of social media.

Be smart about your posts. Don't just post an article. Make a comment about the relevance of that piece. People are busy and they will not spend the extra 5 minutes to read the entire article. Point them to the place you think is relevant and if they find it interesting, they will read the rest of the article. Rest assured; they will remember that *you* pointed them to that important information.

Outlook can also be a huge effectiveness booster in addition to a substantial time-saver. Unless your firm has a proprietary equivalent, Outlook is one of your best choices for keeping track of recurring tasks and events. This is an excellent tool for scheduling client and prospect calls and ensuring that nothing falls through the cracks.

Often advisors feel they can't spare the time to learn new technology. My son said it best when he emphatically told me that not staying up with technology these days is equivalent to being illiterate when I was a kid. From the mouths of babes! Take the time to learn new technology and expand capacity in your business.

Client Service

The most important factor to consider when establishing your client service model is your ability to maintain it regardless of whatever is going on in the markets, your firm, your branch and your life. I cover client service in depth in Chapter 6 but a good starting point is examining what you currently do for each tier of client. Determine what you'd like to do more of or less of for each client tier. Be sure to include soft touches. Never underestimate the power of these touches. They let a client know that you understand and appreciate them as a person.

What's a soft touch? Just checking in. The last conversation you had may have been about a birthday or an important event in their life. Ask them about it and you will be surprised how meaningful that conversation is and how much it means to them.

An easy way to put soft touches on auto is by setting Google alerts for your **top clients' interests, hobbies, or companies.** Google will send you an email when there's news on any of these and you can forward it with a personal note to your client. Often, they will remember these soft touches long after they've forgotten their most recent performance figures.

A few years ago, I had someone influential come up on my Google alerts. There was a story about he and his family running the Chicago marathon. He had run it about a half-dozen times and now his wife and son were running it so all three were going to run it together. I emailed him the article and told him that I was proud of their accomplishment. He emailed me back and asked me how I came across the article. I nonchalantly told him that I just know stuff. He called me and was shocked that I knew that and asked me how I came across the article. Finally, I let him know that I had a Google alert for his

---

name. He was impressed that I took the time to do that for him.

Another small example happened when I sent an article to a client about a Model T Ford car that sold at auction for a record amount. At some point in the past, he had mentioned to me that he collected Model T cars and he liked to restore and sell them. He was touched that I thought about him and it took me a minute to share the story with him.

Referrals

Many advisors are under the mistaken impression that if they just do a good job for their clients, the referral floodgates will open and they'll never have to prospect again. This my friends, is what I call "urban myth." Unfortunately, most clients would have to have someone come up to them on the street and say, "I just won the lottery. Who's your financial advisor?" for them to even think in terms of referrals. Unless they've been in sales before, clients don't think about them.

There is probably no subject more debated in the industry than that of referrals. Asking for referrals in the traditional sense is not always effective either. Think about it. When you ask someone for a referral, you're asking them to think up somebody on the spur of the moment with little or no idea of what you're actually looking for in a referral. It's awkward for you and the client, which means chances are you aren't going to ask. If you do, the referral you get rarely leads to an ideal client.

So, what do you do about this referral dilemma? I've been in the business for a long time and seen advisors use many different methods to build a steady referral business. If you do enough of anything, you will eventually get some results. However, there is an easier way to gain a relatively steady stream of referrals on a consistent basis.

1. **Referral Conditioning:** The answer really is two-fold. The first step is to begin to condition clients to think in terms of referrals. Most advisors have never properly conditioned their clients to think

about referrals. One way to begin to condition clients for referrals is by simply sending a carefully worded referral letter. You do this not because you expect to get a barrage of referrals. You do it because you want to plant the referral seed in the mind of the client in a non-threatening manner. The referral letter accomplishes this quite nicely. Even if they scan the letter and throw it in the trash, it has still accomplished its objective. It has planted the seed that you want and expect referrals. You may have a couple of referrals trickle in as a result of the letter, which is great, but remember that's not its real purpose.

2. **Referral Process Explained:** This is another powerful referral conditioning technique. You'll walk a client through this process once a year at the end of an annual review. There are three primary objections clients have to giving referrals. The first is they're afraid you're going to lose the person money and they'll feel

responsible. There's really not much we can do about that one. Maybe you will; hopefully, you won't. The second is they're afraid you're going to hound the person and the referral won't appreciate them giving you their name. Finally, they worry about confidentiality. They're afraid you may talk to the referral about their investments. If you could eliminate two out of the three primary reasons for not giving referrals before they even happen, do you think your quality and quantity of referrals would go up? You bet they would.

This is exactly what the Referral Process Explained is designed to do. You use it as a "by the way" statement at the end of your review:

"By the way Mr. Client, I'd like to take just a minute to walk you through my referral process so you're comfortable with it, and I can answer any questions you have."

You explain your referral process within the context of answering those two objections—not hounding the person and addressing their confidentiality issues. Every advisor is different with a different style but the following is an example you can modify to fit you:

"When a client gives me a referral, I begin by emailing the referral to let them know who I am, who referred me, and that I'll be calling in the next day or two. When I call the person you refer, I find out more about them and explain my planning process and if we're a good fit, we set an appointment. If we're not, I make a couple of suggestions that I feel could improve their situation. I usually ask if I can send them some information from time to time via email. If they say yes, I thank them and do just that. If they say no—they will never hear from me again. When they come in for the appointment, we begin the planning process. And of course, just like all my clients, everything

is strictly confidential. Is that a process you're comfortable with? Can I answer any questions for you?"

Now let's take a look at everything you accomplish in this power minute. First of all, you planted the seed that you want and expect referrals in the mind of the client, which was your primary objective. You also knocked out two of three major objections to referrals before they even happen. You also let them know that you don't necessarily take every referral you get but even if they don't become a client, you're offering suggestions that could improve their situation. This is a goodwill gesture and lets your client know that the person they've referred will get some guidance from you regardless of whether they become a client or not. This can also cut down on the times you're forced to take a bad referral from a good client. You accomplish a lot and overcome obstacles to referrals in a one-minute "by the way" statement.

Referral Process Explained is a powerful referral conditioning technique. You will only use this technique with the clients you'd like to duplicate and those that you know have good referral potential.

3. **Referral Detective Strategy©:** This is the proactive piece of your referral equation. Advisors typically have radar when it comes to investment or business-related conversations and a potential prospect is mentioned. However, many good potential prospects are often mentioned but overlooked because they didn't come up in a business-related conversation. Referral Detective is a tool to capture these.

    Referral Detective is incredibly simple and low-tech. It doesn't take any additional time. All you have to do is develop good listening skills and your Referral Detective Notebook. Here's how it works. When you're talking with anyone on any subject, pay attention to the people they mention within the course of the conversation. As soon as you can, record them in your notebook. This should be a checkbook-size or pocket calendar-size notebook with blank pages. Each entry should consist of the date of the conversation, the source (the person you're in a conversation with) and any notes you have about the entry. You don't even need a proper name. All you need is enough in your notes that when you go back to your source for an introduction, they'll know who you're talking about.

You'll collect entries all month long. Record every entry you hear whether you think they have potential or not. Then once a month, you put together your Referral Detective Hit List for the upcoming month. These are the people you feel have the most potential. You'll make that judgement call based on your notes and also on the quality of the source.

Referral Detective is effective because "birds of a feather, flock together." If you're talking to a million-dollar client and he mentions he did something with a buddy of his, chances are that person is fairly close to his own socio-economic status. When you're putting together your Hit List, first choose the entries that came from people you'd like to duplicate in your book. Delete the ones you feel have no potential.

For entries that don't make your hit list, but may have potential, reach out to the source and ask if they would mind if you sent the person a LinkedIn connection request. I suggest you filter these people through LinkedIn rather than email because most people still open and read LinkedIn messages while your email could get caught in spam or be ignored. Most people will say yes because it's not as personal of a request as asking for an email address. Another reason this is a better method is because once you get their permission, the source is no longer in the picture. If the referral becomes a connection, you can deal with them directly without having to do that delicate dance with the person referring.

For the entries that make your Hit List, you are going to ask for an introduction. I usually tall advisors to simply ask the source if they think your entry is someone you should get to know. They'll usually tell you the truth. You want to put the source in an advisory role on how to best to reach the person. I would suggest you try to set up the meeting around a fun event like golf, fishing, or a spa day so you're meeting the referral in a casual and relaxed environment. Again, you want to establish your own rapport with the person so after the meeting, you are free to deal with them directly without having to go through the source.

Introductions are far more valuable than referrals. When someone thinks enough of you to give you an introduction, they have a vested interested in selling you to the other person because they only look good if you look good. On the other hand, when your client gives you a referral, that's where it ends. You may or may not ever meet that person for a variety of reasons. **This strategy has proven far more effective than randomly asking people for referrals or simply taking what comes.**

If you've ever received a referral from a new client, you know it's a magical moment. Contrary to what you may believe, this isn't a fluke or a "unicorn sighting moment." This happens for a very specific reason. People refer to you when they feel they are receiving something of value from you. When you demonstrate your value by helping them, they are more likely to refer someone to you. This happens a lot when you are bringing on a new client, but it can also happen during regular reviews, presentation of new ideas, or check-ins during volatile markets. Look for opportunities to make your value obvious to clients.

Branding

Conditioning your clients to think in terms of referrals is only part of the equation. You also want to condition them to say the right things to potential referrals.

Branding is largely a function of repetition. "15 minutes can save you 15% or more on car insurance." That's not exactly a catchy phrase but we've heard it so many times—when we hear it, we immediately think of Geico.

You want to do the same thing for your business. Decide what you want your clients to remember most about you and communicate to others. Keep your branding statement to just a few words and then use that phrase in everything you do.

You want to get clients to the point that when they're talking to friends and the subject of investments comes up, they repeat your branding statement without even thinking about it because that's what they associate with you.

Give this some thought and try it out. Be sure it works for you. The greatest branding statement in the world won't work if you don't use it. Work with your branding statement until it feels comfortable and eventually, a part of you.

The Plan

1. **Information Gathering:** One of the biggest challenges advisors face when creating financial plans is getting the information they need to run the plan in a timely manner. You gain far more complete information more quickly if you take the time to fill out the planning questionnaire with your client. You also significantly increase the likelihood of getting more complete information the first time by sending an appointment confirmation letter, which lists everything they should bring with them to the planning meeting.

2. **Presenting the Plan:** Financial planning can be an overwhelming process to some clients. Begin with what clients are most

interested in—how much they'll need for the retirement they aspire to and their probability of achieving that goal within their desired timeframe. Have an in-depth discussion with them on this and touch on any red flags you discovered after reviewing their plan.

3. **Breaking It Down into Bite-sized Modules:** Explain to clients that there are several areas that you'll be working through with them over time: Social Security, healthcare, beneficiaries, insurance, retirement accounts, and any other areas you feel are important components of their comprehensive financial plan. Break these other areas into modules that you present to them over time. This allows you to add value on an ongoing basis in areas the client doesn't really expect help from you. They begin to see that you have a systematic process rather than a random or piecemeal approach to their investments.

I call this process "layering" because you are adding new layers to their plan as you introduce new goals to the plan. For example, they may have come to you for a very specific need like retirement planning. You begin the relationship by addressing that need and back up your advice using financial planning software. Now that they are working with you and they have a level of trust, you layer on another one of their goals, like education funding. Over time, you will cover all their goals and it is a manageable process for both you and them.

As they see the process unfold over time, they'll become more and more focused on their plan, which is exactly what you want. No one wants to live and die by performance. You want to consciously condition your clients to the point that when the market does anything crazy, they immediately ask you not about their performance but rather, how it effects their plan.

The Investment Management Process

Just like building your success ritual was a very personal step, so too, is structuring your investment management process. Here are some general guidelines.

1. **Build your Investment Matrix**
    - Pick two primary holdings in each primary style—Large Cap, Mid Cap, Small cap—Value, Growth & Balanced in each
    - Choose investments in secondary & satellite styles—REITS, alternatives, sector funds, international

2. **Build Your Platform Model**
    - Establish breakpoints for small, mid-size, and large accounts
    - Decide on the platforms you'll use with each tier of account

3. **Build Your Risk-Based Model Portfolios**
   - Create asset allocation models for each risk profile
   - Build your model portfolios by using the managers within your Investment Matrix to implement your asset allocation models

4. **Build Your Pricing Matrix**
   - Make your pricing fair to the client, an accurate reflection of the value you bring to the client and a pricing structure with which you feel comfortable.
   - Develop conviction that you are worth every penny and be worth every penny
   - Look for methods or articles that help you quantify your value.

5. **Implementation**
   - Use your new business model with all new clients without exception

- For existing clients, begin the transition to your new model with IRAs because there are no tax ramifications to consider

Business Development

Business Development is the lifeblood of your business. Yet, it is always the first component to get squeezed out when markets become volatile or times get crazy. One of the best things you can do for your business is to commit to engaging in some sort of business development activity every week.

You would not believe how many times I ask advisors about their pipeline and get a blank stare or a quick change of subject. It's important that you make it a habit to always know the status of your pipeline. Let's face it. There are a lot of emotional ups and downs inherent in the prospecting process. The larger your pipeline, the smoother these are. When you have a healthy pipeline and someone drops out, it's not the end of the world. However, if you only have two or three prospects in your pipeline and someone drops out, it can be devastating. Consider a robust pipeline an insurance policy that protects you from the bipolar nature of prospecting.

As I mentioned in the "Time Management" section of this chapter, it's best to have one day completely dedicated to business development each week. This ensures that some business development activity will actually happen each week. This puts you immediately ahead of many advisors who engage in little or no business development activities for months at a time.

I also recommend that you disguise your business development activities as fun as often as possible. Hobbies are a great area to look at. People are passionate about their hobbies and a shared interest can break down defense barriers very quickly. Develop a highly structured business development system around your hobby.

For instance, say you're a golfer and want to use golf as a tool to build your business. Playing golf once or twice a week is a great start, but you're just playing if you're not following a system for moving them through your pipeline consistently and effectively. It doesn't have to be complicated and it should appear perfectly natural to the prospect.

Here's one example of a business development system centered around golf that an advisor I know has used very successfully for many years.

- Play as a single.
- Develop relationships, listen well, begin to qualify while on the course.
- Exchange contact information with players with whom you built rapport believe could be qualified.
- Add to prospect list and golf drip system.
- One Week Later: Call to hit a bucket of balls at the driving range.
- Got to the clubhouse after—build rapport.
- Two Weeks Later: Call to play again.
- Mention having lunch sometime.
- Two Weeks Later: Call for lunch.
- Primary Objective for Lunch: Further qualification; Discover pain points and what they're most concerned about in

> the markets or their portfolio right now; Trial close for an appointment.

- If no, find out if you can send them some info on pain point via email if you come across anything, put them on Driving Range/Game rotation schedule.
- Once a quarter, have some sort of business or investment-related conversation, or invite them to an event.

The most important aspect of a successful business development system is it must give you a clearly defined, repeatable structure for working prospects through your pipeline. Having a structure behind your business development activities makes them much easier to implement and maintain consistently. Focusing on something you enjoy doing increases the probability that you will actually engage in them long-term.

If you're out of prospecting shape and don't know where to begin to build your pipeline, begin by building a warm pipeline in a weekend.

When you're new in the business, one of the first things most training programs have you do is build out a warm pipeline. Unfortunately, when you're young and relatively new in the business, you might be hard-pressed to come up with a warm list of qualified prospects.

Unfortunately, this is an exercise that most advisors don't revisit later in their careers when they could build a much more substantial list because they come in contact with more qualified contacts. Keep in mind when you build your warm list that these people don't have to be your best friends. The only criteria you should use to build your list is: you have a reason to believe they may be qualified, and they would recognize your name if they heard or saw it.

Tracking

You can't win the game if you don't know the score on a daily, weekly, and monthly basis. It's important to have a tracking system so you know what's actually going on. What advisors think they're doing and what they are actually doing are often two completely different things. This is why it's important that you have a tracking system for tracking your most results-oriented tasks.

1. **Always track Activities not Results:** Be confident that when you're engaging in the right activities, the results will surely follow. You track activity because it's something that you have complete and total control over.

2. **Track Results-Oriented Activities:** Remember the old 80/20 rule. 80% of your results come from 20% of your activities. Track only your most results-oriented activities.

3. **Decide on your Preferred Method of Tracking:** Decide on a vehicle for your tracking. It can be as simple as a form you develop, print out and complete throughout the day. It can be a spreadsheet or any other program you choose to use. Your method of tracking must be in a form you will actually use

daily. If you don't own it, it won't matter as much to you.

These are the most important systems you must develop in your business to break through plateaus and reach higher levels of production and success. So, where do you begin?

Start by building the system that you feel would have the greatest impact on your business. **Consider what would work for you and what you would actually work on an ongoing basis.** Outline what the system would look like and how it would work. Develop the entire system before you begin the implementation phase. During implementation, allow for a period of adjustment and troubleshooting to make changes as necessary.

These systems will require time to build and diligence to implement. You can build them now or wait until you're forced to build them later. **The ROI relative to time spent building these systems is exponential and worth every minute of effort.** It's one of the best things you can do for your clients, your business and yourself.

Chapter 4 Action Steps

1. Take a good look at your calendar and see if you can "block by day" and put all of your introductory meetings on one day, your discovery meetings on one day, your service meetings on one day, and your closing meetings on one day. This will increase your "batting average."

2. Make it a habit to do your "to-do" list for tomorrow every day before leaving the office. It takes about three months to make it a habit.

3. Look for moments where your clients see your value and directly ask them for a referral. Remember, when they see value, they are most likely to refer.

4. I used a golf strategy for business development, but you can use this for any business development strategy. Take a moment to build out a strategic business

development plan around an activity that you enjoy doing.

5. Create a scorecard to help you track your results. This will allow you to glance at your activity and see exactly how you are doing.

www.eliasrdau.com
me@eliasrdau.com

CHAPTER 5

Using Technology to Your Advantage

"Any sufficiently advanced technology is indistinguishable from magic."
— Arthur C. Clarke

Your ability to leverage your existing book for more assets, revenue, and referrals is directly proportional to the quality of your client service strategy. Building a solid service strategy is the foundation of your business and it begins with knowing exactly who's who in your book.

Advisors always think they know their book—that is, until I have them work through a comprehensive segmentation of their book. This process entails more than just ranking clients based on assets and revenue alone.

When clients see the value you bring to them, they are more likely to refer their friends and family to you. Your value is most evident when you implement a structured client service process.

I once had a coaching conversation with an assistant to an advisor. The advisor was with me to help him make his practice more efficient and get him to the next level. When the assistant and I spoke, he asked how he could help his advisor make more money. I told him the biggest thing he could do was to help his advisor clarify the value and benefits of working with their team.

The assistant looked at me perplexed. I told him to try to create scalable and repeatable systems that will help clients feel like they are receiving personalized and consistent service. The *experience* was truly important, and he needed to find out creative ways to help the client feel special while also making the process repeatable and scalable.

Book Segmentation

How well do you really know your book of business? Your ability to leverage your existing book for more assets, revenue and referrals is directly proportional to the quality of your client service model. Building a solid service strategy is the foundation of your business and it begins with knowing exactly who's who in your book.

A truly comprehensive segmentation of your book entails analyzing not only assets and revenue but also certain intangibles, which are essential to a deep understanding of your book and its potential. The intangibles you consider should reflect your style and the type of business you do but consider asking yourself the following questions when segmenting the book.

- Do you enjoy working with them?
- Have they given you referrals in the past?
- Are they an advocate?
- What is there Center of Influence

potential?

- What is there future revenue potential?

One of the best ways I've seen to quantify your results and get a more accurate assessment of who's who in your book is to use a simple point system like the one outlined in Financial Advisor Coach, Erin Tamberella's book, *Plateau to Pinnacle*. The system gives you structure but is flexible at the same time.

She suggests establishing four breakpoints each for both assets and revenue. These should reflect the nature of your book. If you're just starting out, your top breakpoint might be $500,000 and above for assets and $5,000 a year for revenue. If you're more established in your business, you might set your top breakpoint at $1,000,000 and above for assets and $10,000 and above on revenue.

Next assign a point value to each breakpoint. For instance, you may assign 4 points to clients with assets of $1,000,000 and above, 3 points for assets of $500,000-$999,999, 2 points for assets $250,000-$499,000 and 1 point for assets under $250,000. Do the same for your revenue breakpoints.

Once you've assigned points to each client based on assets and revenue, you'll want to do the same with the intangibles. Assign a 1 or a 0 for yes or no questions. For revenue and Center of Influence questions, you may want to assign a 2, 1 or 0 to more accurately reflect future potential in these areas.

When you're done with the intangibles, add up the points for each client and assign tiers based on point totals. Look at what a perfect score would be and work back from there. For example, let's say, a perfect intangible score was 7 and a perfect assets and revenue score was 8. You may decide 12-15 points is an A client,

Tamberella recommends including a B+ tier when segmenting a book. Often, this can be a sweet spot in an advisor's book. A clients are always taken care of and B clients are typically fairly low-maintenance. Filter off the top point scoring clients in your B tier and put them in your B+ tier.

These should be clients who had a top score on future revenue potential, COI potential, or both. It's also preferable that they scored a 1 on the "do you enjoy working with them" question.

B+ clients are the clients who have the greatest probability of moving up to A client status given the right set of circumstances. When you develop your client service strategy, you'll treat them as A clients.

As you work through your book segmentation, be aware of any common denominators. Even two clients in the same neighborhood, working for the same company, or with the same hobby can be the beginning of a client niche you may be able to develop.

Plan on doing a comprehensive segmentation of your book once a year. Circumstances often change over the course of a year. You want to ensure that no new client is overlooked and everyone is still in their appropriate tier.

Your Client Service Strategy

Begin to create your client service model by examining what you're currently doing for clients in terms of contact and service. Because client service is the foundation of your business, it's important that you be brutally honest and ask yourself the following questions:

- What are you currently doing now for clients in terms of service: phone calls, emails, reviews, events, meals with clients, birthdays, anniversaries, when they give you a referral?
- What are your strengths and weaknesses in these areas?
- What would you like to be doing more of in terms of client service?
- What would you like to be doing less of?
- Do you have a "surprise and delight" component to your service model? This is extremely important and often overlooked by advisors. Remember, clients will remember personalized soft touches long after they've forgotten about their latest performance. It's also one of the best ways you have of generating unsolicited positive word-of-mouth praise for yourself and your business.

Do you know your A and B+ clients well enough to bring a personalized "surprise and delight" element to the relationship? If not, I strongly suggest you develop a methodical system for getting to know your clients on a more personal basis. This is how you build deep relationships.

- What could you add to or modify in your service model that might forge a deeper relationship with your clients?

- Do your clients feel like you take care of them, look out for them, have their best interests in mind, and they can trust you? These are the feelings you want to nurture in clients and your client service model is a primary tool for doing so.

Allocate the time necessary to really think about these questions. Use your answers as a guide to developing a client service strategy that will help you build closer client relationships. The most important criteria for your client service model is that you must be able to maintain it no matter what is happening in the markets, the world, your firm and your life. Remember, consistency is sign of a strong business.

Once you've developed your client service strategy, you'll want to automate the process as much as possible. Create a calendar of repeating tasks for each household in your book. Ideally, you want a system that allows you to schedule and receive notifications at the beginning of each week for every call and contact you need to make and every appointment that should be set. You want to create a system that you have to think little about once it's set it up, one that prevents client contact from falling through the cracks. Client contact is the lifeblood of your business.

Salesforce Action Plans

Salesforce is one of the most powerful CRM platforms available today. Salesforce Action Plans are great for streamlining recurring processes for maximum effectiveness. Let's say that you developed a specific onboarding process for new clients which consists of a series of tasks.

You can create a task series template for your onboarding process in Salesforce. Once it's created, you can apply this template each time this series of tasks is required when onboarding in the future.

Depending on the version of Salesforce you're using, you can create Action Plans in Salesforce for the following:

- Accounts
- Contacts
- Leads
- Opportunities
- Campaigns
- Cases

Use every opportunity you have to utilize technology to automate processes and increase your effectiveness. If you have access to Salesforce, take some time each week to learn the program. It can save you a lot of time by automating many of your systems and processes. The more automated your tasks can be, the more professional you will look and feel.

For example, you may want to automate your new client onboarding by creating a 90-Day Action Plan. You can automatically assign tasks to your staff and yourself each day. For example, one day after you meet with them, you send a handwritten note. Two days after you meet, a member of your team calls to welcome them on board. Five days later someone checks on the asset transfer. 45 days after they open the account, you set a meeting to go through their new statements. You get the idea. This helps you to create a memorable experience for the new clients.

Google Alerts

Google Alerts are another great technology tool for helping you add the special personal touch that people will remember. You can set parameters and Google will notify when stories appear on the subject. You can set a Google Alert for almost anything but here are some examples of alerts you may considering setting for top clients:

People (prospects and clients)
Groups (NAWBO, Chamber of Commerce)

Companies (large local employers, companies your clients work at)

Layoffs (local companies)

Places (your hometown, towns you prospect in)

When you receive a Google Alert, read the article. If it's appropriate email the link to your client or prospect with a personal note. They'll be impressed because you listened and are attentive but also because you took the time to recognize them or their situation.

Good social currency policy is to give before you ask for anything in return. This is an important concept. If you truly grasp the significance of developing and maintaining this mentality, it will serve you well throughout your career—and maybe even keep you humble.

Why You Must Keep Good Notes

Arbitrations are the stuff of advisor nightmares! If you've ever had the unfortunate experience of being involved in one, you know firsthand, that the notes you keep can make you or break you. If it isn't documented, it never happened. Think about that for a moment.

Something I've learned over the years is that a complaint or lawsuit can happen to any advisor at any time by any client over anything. No one is immune. This is why it's so important that you document every single conversation you have with every single client.

This practice is not unique to our industry. My wife, Tracy, works in the Emergency Room. All their charts are electronic and they cannot discharge a patient if there are not adequate notes in their chart. A minimum standard of care must be documented in the notes or they are not allowed to close a chart and let the client go home.

And, I don't consider, "talked to clients and everything is fine" adequate. When adding your notes to the system always ask yourself what you'd want to have in those notes about that conversation if those notes were your primary defense in an arbitration with this client.

This may seem extreme, but I want you to be protected if they unthinkable would ever happen and you found yourself in an arbitration. Also, maintaining good notes also helps you to remember conversations and better service your clients.

A good advisor is a partner to their clients. Remember, to always use the term "we" whenever possible. It reinforces in your own mind and the client's or prospect's that you are a team.

This is exactly how you want to be perceived and build the dynamics of your relationship with the client.

Finally, you may want to consider implementing what I call a, "Playback" to your clients and prospects. This is where you send them a copy of your notes and what you understand about them. Clients love this because they know you were listening, and they appreciate that you asked for their validation. It also gives your clients and prospects the ability to clarify a point you shared with them in your Playback. I also make it a point at the end of every client meeting to ask this simple question:

"When I go back to my office and go through everything we covered today, I want to make sure I address your concerns. Please tell me the

top three things you need me to address before we meet again."

This tactic is so simple but it helps tremendously in guiding you and your advice. Clients will tell you EXACTLY what they want you to address. I've implemented it into every client conversation. It's a great way to end the meeting and the clients know that you care about them.

Chapter 5 Action Steps

1. Print out your entire book of business. Don't worry about your firm. I've heard countless advisors say that if they print their entire book of business their manager would accuse them of wanting to leave. *But*...they only have a reason to question you if you leave soon after you printed out your entire book!

2. Create a formula that you believe is right to segment your clients. Ask yourself the five questions I highlight at the beginning of the chapter to give yourself a true representation of your best clients and future best clients. Keep in mind that there will be people you enjoy talking to but who don't really contribute to your business. There are others that are great at referring the right clients to you but don't generate much revenue.

3. Make a list of clients that you can partner with another advisor on who can service

them and retain them. You never know who may win the lottery or receive an inheritance from a wealthy relative!

4. Identify your B+ clients because these are the clients that will help you get to the next level. They can really propel your business!

5. Take in an inventory of the current technology that is helping you deliver on your service strategy and decide what to get rid of, keep and acquire to help you become more efficient.

6. When it comes to notes, make sure you are keeping detailed notes. Cell phones and tablets help you dictate your notes so it should no longer be a tedious task. Do it right away and you will capture the essence of your conversations. You never know when you will need that information again.

7. Try putting in a few Google alerts on your own. Search for your alma mater, your favorite sports teams, or even a company you like. It is fun to see the daily news in your inbox about the things you care about.

ELIAS R. DAU, CRPC®

• C H A P T E R   6 •

Renters vs. Owners: How to Properly Build a Team

"The strength of the team is each individual member. The strength of each member is the team."

— Phil Jackson

In your early career as a financial advisor, time is not an issue because you don't yet have a lot of clients to service. Although you're handling everything yourself, you still have ample time to market, build your business, and service new clients as they come aboard. However, as you grow, the amount of time you have to devote to these important aspects of your business begins to dwindle and growth can slow substantially.

Technology can carry you for a while, but eventually, when you've exhausted all available resources and delegated everything possible, it's time to give some serious thought as to how you want to grow and expand your business going forward. Regardless of what type of partnership arrangement you choose to pursue, partnering is not something to be taken lightly.

You would think long and hard before you ever considered marriage. The same careful thought and consideration must go into choosing the right partner to share your business with if the partnership is to be successful. For a marriage or partnership to succeed, you and your partner must share similar values, goals and ideology on how you wish to progress moving forward.

Allocate some alone time away for power-thinking on your business at an off-sight location—not at the office and not at home. Choose a place where you can get away from all of your everyday stressors for a while, even if it's just for the evening.

Check into a local Airbnb for the night or a weekend if you can swing it. Put your phone on Do Not Disturb and unplug from all email and social media. Until you take the time to do this on occasion, you cannot begin to grasp how much of a distraction your electronic devices actually are. I know when I unplug (not often enough), I'm amazed at how much time seems to instantly materialize in my day or evening.

Start with the end in mind. Begin by asking yourself the following questions:

- What does your ideal business look like now?
- What would it look like in 3 years, 5 years, 10 years?
- What do you enjoy doing the most in your business?
- What do you enjoy doing the least?
- What aspects of the business are you best at?
- Where are your weakest links in your business?

What are your goals for your business?

- How much do you want to work?
- How long do you want to work?
- At the current time, would you and your business benefit more from a vertical or horizontal partnership arrangement?
- What do you hope to accomplish by taking on a partner?
- What role would you like to see your partner own?
- What specific skillset do you want your partner to have?
- What personality traits are most important to you in a partner?
- What personality traits in your partner are non-negotiable?

Consider these questions carefully and write down your answers. Tweak your answers until they are as specific and detailed as possible. Take the time to evaluate and process your thoughts before taking any next steps.

Vertical vs. Horizontal Team

In general, the shorter the time period you're planning for, the more accurate your planning will be. I suggest to my advisors that they do tactical planning for their business in 3-5-year time spans. It becomes difficult to do meaningful tactical planning ten years out because so much can change.

However, you should plan on revisiting your long-term strategic goals once a year. It's good for the soul to stay connected to your long-term vision. It's also a great way to gauge how well your short-term tactical steps are supporting your long-term vision.

One of the first decisions you have to make is whether building a vertical or horizontal team is a better fit for your business right now. You may choose to build your team one way initially and then round it out by going the other direction later. Neither is right or wrong.

A vertical team has a single financial advisor at the top. Everyone else is an employee. All of the revenue goes to the advisor who is responsible for compensating the rest of the team. This is actually a less complicated structure because all decisions are made by the advisor without a multitude of opinions with which to contend. The downside to this arrangement is there's no intellectual or emotional synergy inherent in the partnership.

Vertical Team

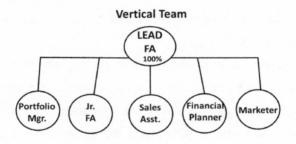

A horizontal team is what we usually think of when we think of a partnership. It's more of a true partnership. Revenue and expenses are divided among the partners. Synergy and equity is shared but with that comes an increased probability of conflicts arising over the direction of the business.

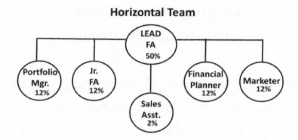

Horizontal Team

Once you've decided on which team structure will serve your business best, your next step is to begin defining roles and responsibilities. The clearer you are on this, the easier it becomes to find the right partner for your business.

Do your due diligence. This is an important decision in your career. You want perfect clarity on your personal and business goals and be able to articulate these clearly to all potential partners. If you decide to build a horizontal team, evaluate your potential partner's client relationships and business philosophy to be certain they are compatible with your own

Bringing on Another Financial Advisor

Developing a successful partnership takes time. There are advantages to bringing on a partner. The most significant is the potential to build a larger business together than either of you could build alone. Economies of scale free up time for each partner to do more of what they do best and enjoy the most. This alone can be a productivity amplifier.

One of the most important things to remember when searching for a partner is to look for an advisor with a skillset that is *complimentary* to your own. All too often I see advisors gravitate toward potential partners who are exactly like them. Initially, this may feel comfortable but ultimately, it can be an impediment to your growth.

You tend to excel at the tasks you enjoy the most. By pursuing a complimentary skillset, not only are you able to fill in gaps in your current business but you're free to do more of what you enjoy and are best at. When partners are able to engage in these activities more often and for longer periods of time, the business grows exponentially.

You'll want to evaluate your personality styles, business styles, expectations, and primary motivators. According to Michael Kitces, well-known financial planner, speaker and blogger, "Differences in behavior and work styles are a challenge that can be solved with better communication (and understanding each other's communication style), but fundamental differences in primary motivators are significantly harder to reconcile and are more likely to lead to conflict that can undermine or entirely disintegrate a business partnership over time."[17]

When you find a potential candidate, it's important that you assess how compatible you are both personally and from a business perspective. Just because you were both successful at building your independent businesses does not necessarily mean you'll be successful or effective working together.

---

[17] Michael Kitces, "Assessing Compatibility To Partner With Another Financial Advisor," July 11, 2016, https://www.kitces.com/blog/financil-advisor-partner-compatability-assessment-from-partnershhip-resource/

Finder, Minder or Grinder

The Finder, Minder, Grinder distinctions are our first step in categorizing roles and responsibilities. Are you a Finder, a Grinder or a Minder? It's important to be brutally honest with yourself as you evaluate your talents in each of these three broad categories. You have to be clear on where you stand before you can begin to look for a partner whose skillset compliments your own.

Finders are the rainmakers. Every business must have at least one. These are the hunters who are motivated by the chase. They find the new clients and business opportunities and close them.

Minders supervise the process and the people. Their energy is focused on nurturing the business internally. They constantly monitor the process and do everything they can to maintain harmony. Their job is to make sure the ship moves in the right direction at the right speed and all systems are go!

Grinders are the ones who make it all happen. They take the team vision and the opportunities delivered by the finders and they execute. They work relentlessly to deliver the appropriate products and services to clients and the rest of the team.

In the beginning, you wear all three hats in your business but as it grows, you must learn to delegate. This is sometimes a difficult lesson for advisors. However, for you to continue to grow at a sustainable rate, you must delegate the right tasks to the right people.

Roles and Responsibilities

Now it's time to get more specific with roles and responsibilities on the team. We want to not only define them but also generate clear job descriptions for each role. It's also a good idea to include an accountability component. Compensation that links roles and responsibilities to measurable activities along with annual reviews seems to consistently produce the best results among teams.[18]

Begin by brainstorming the roles and responsibilities that fall under the Finder, Grinder, and Minder categories. Once you have an exhaustive list for each, mark off everything that's not applicable to your business. Next pull out the tasks you enjoy doing and are good at. What remains is the start of job descriptions for other team members.

High functioning teams always have systems built into their businesses. The more streamlined and seamless the systems, the more scalable the business is. I suggest you revisit Chapter 4 on systematizing your business with your Finder, Minder, Grinder job description lists in hand. As you review that chapter, you may discover additional tasks you'd like to include under the different categories.

By now, a clearer picture of the financial advisor or team member who would be an ideal addition should be starting to emerge.

[18] David J. Mullen Jr, "Million Dollar Financial Advisor Team," Accessed May 17, 2020, https://books.google.com/books?id=J-hWDwAAQBAJ&newbks=0&printsec=frontcover&pg=PA122&dq=strategic+vs.+tactical+financial+advisor+team&hl=en#v=onepage&q=strategic%20vs.%20tactical%20financial%20advisor%20team&f=false

Remember as you begin your search to seek out people who compliment your skillset not duplicate it.

Renter vs. Owner

When attempting to integrate a partner into your team, you need to determine if they will be a renter or an owner on your team. Look at it from their vantage point and clarify what their objectives are for joining the team. A "renter" will be there for a set amount of hours. They are usually compensated by salary or an hourly compensation structure. If you call them on the weekend, they may not answer or call you back until Monday. They are important to the team but they have a very defined set of responsibilities. For example, some advisors may have a financial planner on the team and they are responsible for the data input, number crunching and analysis. They show up every day at 9am and leave at 5pm. They should be reliable and interested in getting their tasks done.

An "owner" is someone who puts in extra effort for the team. Some or all of their compensation comes directly from the revenues of the business. Part or all their compensation is driven from the growth of the business. They respond to your calls in the evening or over the weekend and they work to build the business. Think of a partner in a law firm. They are responsible for driving revenue and growing the business. Their focus is on the long-term and they are motivated by growth.

Discuss with potential team members' what their long-term vision looks like. Once you're clear on their objectives and expectations, it's much easier to decide on an appropriate compensation structure.

Partnership Integration

The term "partnership" is definitely one that's subject to interpretation. I've seen every conceivable advisor partnership structure you can imagine. Some partnerships are nothing more than two advisors covering for each other when one is out of the office. At the other extreme, I've seen truly integrated partnerships that have mastered role ownership and economies of scale.

Neither is necessarily right or wrong. You must decide what's best for your business. However, keep in mind that for many advisor teams, it's more of an evolutionary process. For this discussion, I'll highlight steps to building a fully integrated team. The same general steps apply regardless of where you rest on the integration spectrum.

It's wise to consider implementing a trial "dating period" where you can work together and see if the two of you are a good fit. Start with a couple clients and add more as you go along. You'll learn more about each other and the synergy you have when working together with clients.

Systems Integration

One of the first things you'll want to do together with a new partner is compare your systems and processes. You do this with the goal of leveraging the best each of you bring to the partnership with regards to the way you conduct business.

For instance, you may have a fantastic client service system while your partner's onboarding process may be far superior to your own. Together with your partner, develop a plan to integrate the best of each into a team process you both are comfortable with and will use.

This is important because you always want to ensure that clients are getting a uniform standard of service, regardless of who the primary advisor is. This becomes much easier if all partners are using the same general processes and systems to conduct business.

Review Chapter 4 again for a refresher on the general systems your business should have in place to operate effectively. Pay attention to the actual structure and logistics of the system. This is where the potential to significantly increase efficiency lies.

Every advisor is different, and every client is different. Going back to our client service example, you may find upon comparing systems, that you call your clients more often than your partner. Each of you know what's right for your respective clients. I'm not proposing that you both have to contact your clients with the same degree of frequency. What I am suggesting is that you both use the same logistical system for ensuring that you both deliver the quality of service best suited to your clients.

Cross-Pollination

I can't tell you how many advisor teams I see whose businesses are completely siloed. Unfortunately, this arrangement negates a lot of the advantages you get with a partnership. Cross-pollination takes time and it's actually a step that you will work on as long as you're in a partnership.

With both existing clients and new clients, some degree of cross-pollination is always good idea. First of all, you're perceived as bigger and more professional when you have a team behind you. This often gives clients more peace of mind. It's better for clients because if you are out, your client isn't talking to a complete stranger. Your partner is at least somewhat familiar with your client's situation.

So how exactly do you cross-pollinate? It's best done in phases. Ideally, you want it to be so subtle, the client is barely aware of the process at all. Your initial step is for each of you to send letters to all of your clients introducing your partner and briefly outlining how the new team will benefit the client.

The next phase involves simply introducing your partner when clients come in the office. This should be very casual—just a brief introduction and hello. From that point, slowly step up the engagement. Your next step may be for you and your partner to take the client to lunch. After that, you may tell your client you'd like to have your partner sit in on a meeting because of some expertise they have. This stepped-up engagement should take place over a period of one to two years.

You're still the primary on the account. You just want your client to get to the point where they feel comfortable with your partner being involved in their financial planning process.

Division of Labor

At this point, you've integrated your business systems together for maximum efficiency, keeping the best of the best. You've successfully cross-pollinated across and clients are completely comfortable with the team. The final step to a fully integrated team is Division of Labor.

Many teams never reach this phase or choose not to work in this phase. This is fine. Again, you have to do what you feel is best for your clients, your team and you. If your team takes the time to cross-pollinate, you are already well ahead of many advisor teams out there.

In this step, partners gravitate more to the roles and responsibilities they're best at and duplication of tasks across the team is minimized. This represents a giant leap in efficiency.

What this Division of Labor phase actually looks like depends on the nature of your team. This process is best begun in a more casual off-site meeting with no office distractions or phones. Have each team member come to the meeting with their answers to the following questions:

- What roles and responsibilities on the team do they most enjoy?
- What business areas, if a team member were to take ownership of those areas, would benefit the team the most? Why?
- What business area might they be interested in owning?

In your meeting, discuss the answers and formulate a plan for moving forward. I would suggest you also approach this step in phases. Begin with your most pressing business area. Hammer out what the role would look like and create a SOP (Standard Operating Procedure) around the role.

If one partner takes on the role for the team, it's important to discuss what they'll have to give up or modify to create the time needed for the role. Brainstorm among the team on the best way to accomplish this.

Implement one Division of Labor role at a time. Be sure it's fully integrated and functioning seamlessly before repeating the process with another role.

Follow all or some of these steps on your way to a fully integrated team. Even if your team never reaches the Division of Labor step, it's a good idea for all teams to plan some sort of cross-pollination strategy. A strong team is good for the clients and it's good for the advisors.

Internship

Internship programs are popular with financial advisors because they can tap into a pool of educated, driven individuals for minimal cost. An intern can tackle those projects that you'd love to see done but always seem to get put off. It's also a great way to mine for future employees.

You typically have an intern for a period of only a few months so you must have a plan if you hope to maximize your time with them. Here are some tips:

- Prepare a list of exactly what you'd like them to accomplish in their time with you
- Prioritize your list
- Review the list with your assistant and determine what they will have to learn first, second and third if they are to finish all the tasks.
- You should consider giving your intern less tasks and more projects. The last thing you want your intern to do is come to you after each task and ask what's next. Task them with longer-term projects to create some autonomy and begin training them to be creative thinkers.
- Set specific times for them to check in with you. They are excited and they want to give you updates along the way. Just make sure both of you have scheduled times to check in with each other.

Your internship program should be a win-win for both you and the intern. You want them to accomplish the tasks you've assigned to them but you also want them to get a realistic taste of the job. Plan on having them sit in on client meetings. They'll be more invested in their paperwork duties if they can put a face to a name.

Have one team member mentor each intern. For best results, this person should plan on meeting with the intern weekly to review what they accomplished relative to their goals for the week. It's important that the mentor monitor progress on any projects on which the intern is working. This gives them constructive feedback on an ongoing basis and sets them up for success.

Explain how their role is assisting the team or enhancing the overall client experience. This helps them to understand how different facets of the business fit together and better retain what they're learning.

Arrange scheduled times for the intern to shadow the lead advisors. This gives them an opportunity to get a better idea of what the job entails. They also experience different approaches to the business and different styles when dealing with clients.

Always conduct exit interviews. Feedback from the intern will help you improve your internship program in the future and maximize its benefit to the team. Plan on having all team members access the intern's performance and provide input that helps them with progress in their career.

With clients living longer and retiring for longer periods of time, the financial advice they require is becoming more and more complex. A team is often better equipped to handle the varied financial needs of a client and their family over a financial lifetime.

Many clients who have worked with their advisors for a long period of time worry about what will happen to them if their advisor retires, becomes ill, or dies. And their fears are warranted. Recent studies show:

- Over one third of financial advisors plan to leave the business within the next 10 years.

- More than $2.3 trillion in assets are managed by financial advisors who are 60 or older.
- Less than 25% of these advisors have any sort of succession plan.[19]

This represents a huge opportunity for solo advisors and small partnerships. The industry trend toward teaming is not likely to diminish any time soon. Firms will continue to promote teaming as they scramble to retain the assets of aging financial advisors.

---

[19] "Succession Planning for Financial Advisors," *Cuna Mutual Group*, Accessed April 1, 2019, https://www.cunamutual.com/resource-library/insights/operations/succession-planning-for-financial-advisors.

Chapter 6 Action Items

We will finish this chapter with where we started, so I ask you to be honest with yourself and answer these questions:

- What does your ideal business look like now?
- What would it look like in 3 years, 5 years, 10 years?
- What do you enjoy doing the most in your business?
- What do you enjoy doing the least?
- What aspects of the business are you best at?
- Where are your weakest links in your business?
- What are your goals for your business?
- How much do you want to work?
- How long do you want to work?
- At the current time, would you and your business benefit more from a

vertical or horizontal partnership arrangement?

- What do you hope to accomplish by taking on a partner?
- What role would you like to see your partner own?
- What specific skillset do you want your partner to have?
- What personality traits are most important to you in a partner?
- What personality traits in your partner are non-negotiable?

ELIAS R. DAU, CRPC®

Leveraging Your Most Powerful Resource: People

"If I have seen further it is by standing on the shoulders of giants."

— Isaac Newton

Do you know what your clients really want and need from you? Many financial advisors think they already know, but they're not always right. What may seem like a great idea to you may not be something clients and prospects value nearly as much. It's easy to misinterpret what's most important to clients and even worse, make incorrect assumptions about how your brand is perceived locally.

The only way to really know what's important to clients is to ask them. You'll gain insight into your business that you really can't get any other way. Chances are you'll also come away with some fresh ideas that could help your business grow.

In 2013, a Financial Planning Association Research and Practice Institute Practice Management Study found that advisors who employ some sort of client feedback mechanism in their business grow faster. In some cases, that incremental growth can be significant—up to 10-50% more among advisors who solicit feedback from their clients on a consistent basis.[20]

There are many different ways you can institute a feedback platform in your business. One of the best ways you can accomplish this is

---

[20] Grant Hicks, "Why 85% of Financial Advisors Don't Do Feedback," *LinkedIn Pulse,* May 29, 2017, https://www.linkedin.com/pulse/why-85-financial-advisors-dont-do-feedback-grant-hicks/

by creating your own business advisory board. This is simply a group of your best clients and centers of influence who can provide valuable feedback to you on various aspects of your business.

The primary function of the board is to help you understand what's important to clients by seeking their opinions and honest feedback on what you do and how you do it. Keep in mind that you must be open hearing what they have to say. You don't necessarily have to act on every idea you hear but it is important that you acknowledge and validate their opinions and take their feedback under consideration.

Setting Up Your Client Advisory Board

Who you choose to be on your client advisory board is critically important to its success and ultimate value to you. There are many different opinions on the type of people you want to invite to be on the client advisory board.

To some advisors, diversity is important. They strive to develop a board that is representative of a cross-section of their book. When you have gender, racial, age, and occupational diversity on your board, you gain a wide variety of perspectives. All of these demographic factors can influence how people perceive you and their finances.

Other advisors are more concerned with the nature of their relationship with the people on their client advisory board. In this case, you'll want to choose people you know truly care about you and your business. This should include both large and small clients and their willingness to be open and honest with you should be a primary consideration.

You may want to consider both diversity and the nature of your relationship when choosing people to include on your board. However, I believe the most effective client advisory boards are those comprised of people you'd like to clone as clients. The whole point of the board is to help you gain clarity in your marketing and service mix and grow your business with the right kind of clients and centers of influence. It makes sense that your board be comprised of these very people.

Begin by going through your book and find the 10-12 people you'd most like to clone as clients. If your final list is comprised of more than 12 people, choose your top candidates and file the rest of list away for later. When your board becomes a valuable resource in your business, you may want to rotate your membership for fresh ideas every couple of years.

Although your board will likely be heavily weighted with your "best" clients, these aren't always your biggest clients. Choose people who have utilized a wide range of your products and services. Be sure to factor in the intangibles we discussed earlier in the book in the section in Chapter 5 on book segmentation. Questions to ask yourself when choosing your board members are:

- Do you enjoy working with them?
- Do they take your advice?
- Have they given you referrals in the past?
- Are they an advocate?
- What is their future revenue potential?

- What is their COI potential?
- Are they hyper-fee sensitive?

Keep in mind that not everyone on your board must be a client. Although clients should have the strongest presence on your board, it's perfectly fine to include centers of influence with whom you have a strong relationship. I've even heard of advisors who have included a strong prospect or two on their board. It's a great way for substantial prospects to witness the relationship and synergy that exists between you and your clients. Also, prospects often bring a different perspective to the table. If you do choose to include a prospect on your board, this should be someone you have a strong relationship with and meets all the previous criteria discussed.

As I have mentioned previously, my wife works in the Emergency Room and many Emergency Rooms are run by an outside group hired by the ER. I wanted to work with the doctors and staff of the group that my wife worked for.

With my wife's permission, I spoke with one of the principals of the practice and asked him for advice. The line of questions went something like this: What is it that ER doctors need from a financial advisor? How would you want to work with your advisor? Do these particular products and services fit your needs? How do I get in front of ER doctors and staff? It was amazing how this type of questioning helped me craft my message and he became a client. He became not just a client but a raving fan. He has been an advocate for my practice.

Asking him for advice appealed to him psychologically. The doctor whom I had asked for the advice was flattered that I wanted his opinion. He felt obligated to help me and gave me his open and honest feedback. Because he gave me his best feedback, he now had a vested interest in seeing me succeed. He was now a stakeholder in my success. My success became his success and my failure, his failure. Subsequently, he gave me his business and sent me more business because he had a stake in my practice. He still refers business to me and his co-workers will check in when they need financial advice.

Let's not lose sight of the original purpose and that was to get honest and critical feedback on our practice. Be honest about your intention to get feedback and if they do business with you, it's a nice dividend but it cannot be the primary purpose for the Advisory Board relationship.

The ideal number of people on your board depends on your comfort zone and the nature of your business. Most advisors shoot for between 10-12 members on their board. I've seen successful client advisory boards with as few as 6 people on it. However, I'd be hesitant to have more than 12 members because it becomes difficult to manage that many people and give each person adequate time to express their opinions.

Personally, I think the sweet spot for advisory boards in that 6-9 person range. You still get a wide range of opinions and ideas but retain that feeling of intimacy between you and your board.

The Agenda

The whole point of your Client Advisory Board is to provide you with open, honest feedback on your business and service. This is your opportunity to ask clients and COIs anything you want and asking the right questions is essential to a successful outcome.

When you first begin with your board, it's a good idea to focus on gaining clarity and understanding on your current client experience—from the client's perspective. This will give you ideas on how you can improve what you're currently doing. Here are some areas you may wish to address:

- What areas of your existing services do clients value the most?
- What's most important to clients in a business relationship?
- What made them want to do business with you?
- What would they like to see more of from you?
- What would they like to see less of from you?
- What type of client events would they like to see from you over the coming year?

- Where do you think we excel?
- Where could we improve?
- How likely are you to refer friends and family to us? Why or why not?
- What could we do that would make us more referable in your eyes?
- We all do business everywhere. Who do you feel is doing something positive or unique in their business that you really like?

In subsequent board meetings, you can address more specific areas like your marketing plan and their ideas on how to attract more clients. You may even ask them to review your business plan or make suggestions on additional services they would find valuable.

It's important to always use open-ended questions. They'll provide you with the most in-depth answers and potential for elaboration. Closed-end questions are a dead end and provide little in useable information.

Be prepared with follow-up questions to drill down and get specific feedback you can use. For instance, if you ask the board what's most important to them in an advisor relationship, "trust" is probably the most common answer you'll hear. We all know that, but that answer alone gives you little information you can actually use. Follow up questions like what creates trust in their mind can take you past the emotion and lead to more tangible actions steps. It's questions like these that can really help you uncover what aspects of your business are perceived as significant in the eyes of the client.

You should be realistic in the number of questions you can actually cover with the board in a two-hour meeting. The number of people on your board will, in part, dictate this. If you have 10 people on your board, you will likely be limited to two or three questions. It's important that you give everyone adequate time to speak and everyone feels heard.

It's also a good idea to have an agenda with the questions you plan to ask and distribute this to members of your board in advance. It's been my experience that doing so provides additional depth and value to discussion. When it's not done, this suggestion invariably appears in board member evaluation forms. In your agenda, plan on providing a brief but clear description of exactly what their role as a board member will be. This helps you to set and manage expectations from the beginning.

Developing the Right Mindset

It's imperative that you approach your board meetings with the right mindset. For the Client Advisory Board to be effective, members must feel that you're truly interested in what they think and feel. To accomplish this, you must be open-minded and humble. Not everything you hear may be positive. You must be prepared for that and know how you're going to handle it in the meeting.

Remember, you carry no risk in a Client Advisory Board meeting. You're not committed to taking any particular suggestion. Your only commitment is to listen with an open mind and be sure every participant feels heard. Attentive listening is becoming a lost art. When clients feel heard, it honors their opinion.

Pay particular attention to common feedback. Everything expressed in your board meeting is strictly the opinion of participating board members. The opinion of a single member carries far merit than an opinion shared by many of your board members.

If ideas come up that conflict with your current business practices, simply listen. You can always give them consideration later should you choose to do so. It's important that you avoid becoming defensive or provide rationalizations. This will quickly shut down the open conversation you're trying so hard to promote. Prove to your board that they can talk about anything and are free express exactly. When they know you're grateful for their feedback—both good and bad—that's when the advice you receive becomes golden.

Follow-Up

Like most everything in this business, the key to the kingdom lies in your follow-up, which is exactly where most advisors drop the ball.

Appropriate follow-up will help you maximize the effectiveness of your board meetings.

Keep board members informed on activities you plan to explore further as a result of the meeting. This can be as simple as sending them a second copy of the agenda with your Action Steps listed at the bottom. This lets members know that you were listening and that they were heard. It also gives them that positive, goodwill feeling that they were able to help.

Send out a handwritten thank-you note to each board member. In addition to thanking them, be sure to express how much you appreciated their honesty and openness. If appropriate, you may also want to highlight the value of one of their suggestions.

Creating a Client Advisory Board can provide invaluable feedback from the type of clients you trying to attract. Always include people on your board whom you respect and whose opinions you would find most valuable. The insights you gain from this feedback structure will help you grow your business. More importantly, your board members begin to develop a more vested interest in your practice and your success. This is a positive in your business money can't buy.

Chapter 7 Action Steps

1. Identify 10-12 relationships that you want to contact and ask to be on your advisory board.

2. Create talking points about what you want to accomplish with their advice:

   - Communicate the reason why you are asking them to be on the board. Hint* It is because you value their advice.
   - Create an open and honest forum for them to communicate with you.
   - Give them your goals for your practice, up front.
   - Make it fun for them and share some case studies to walk through.
   - Ask them what it is they want from a financial advisor.
   - Reiterate your goals.
   - Ask them to confidentially share what they need from you. This can

be in writing, survey or one on one call.

3. Follow up with a thank you.

4. Follow up with your next meeting. Remember, they are on your board so they will expect follow up and progress checks.

www.eliasrdau.com
me@eliasrdau.com

ELIAS R. DAU, CRPC®

Conclusion

"Diamonds are nothing more than chunks of coal that stuck to their jobs."

— Malcolm Forbes

I wrote this book to help you systematize the important aspects of your business, increase efficiency, and, as a result, increase your assets, revenue, and referrals. Follow the concepts and Action Steps in this book and it will help you reach your goals faster, easier, and with less stress regardless of what's going on around you in the markets, your firm, or your branch.

I come to the end of this book just as the second wave of Covid-19 is ramping up. One important concept I'd like you to take with you from this book is that **it is much easier to build your book in challenging markets than it is in good ones.**

When the markets are going straight up and people are making money, there is very little incentive for prospects to change. However, when clients and prospects start to feel the pain of volatile and uncertain markets, they are looking for answers and a better way. In other words, they are hungry for change so they're willing to listen and hear what you have to say.

Seize this opportunity! When any difficult market begins, advisors are usually very good at contacting clients and keeping them informed. However, the longer the downturn persists, the more client contact begins to drop off. This is a time when you can swoop in and become the hero to many of these prospects. Remember, this is precisely when they're feeling the pain and searching for new ideas.

When other advisors are slacking off of client contact, step up yours with both clients and prospects. Ask them what they're most concerned about right now. This gives you a strong indication of what their hot buttons are, and it's your opportunity to demonstrate value. Become a valuable resource to them in difficult times and you'll get new clients and hold onto your existing ones.

With every challenge in our business lies the seeds of great opportunity. Be the contrarian and train yourself to see those opportunities when other advisors only see problems and challenges. This is a "contact" sport. Your ability to leverage your existing book for more assets and revenue begins and ends with your client contact system. Likewise, your ability bring in new assets and relationships begins and ends with prospect contact and your business development strategy. In the end contact is your "superpower."

Systems are the foundation of your business. You can build them now or you can build them later but sooner or later you have to build them if you want your business to grow and thrive. The Action Steps at the end of every chapter will get you started on your way to building clearly defined, repeatable systems for your business.

Regardless of whether you want to grow or just have more life balance, creating these systems will make you look and feel more professional. Your clients will feel taken care of and informed which makes you more referable. The more referable you are, the faster your business grows and the faster it grows, the more time you'll have to do what is important to you.

The systems you create for your business also add something to your business that all successful enterprises have: consistency. Consistency in your business means clients and prospects can count on you to do what you say you will do. They get meaningful and consistent information from you because you have a system for that and when times are volatile, your contact with clients and prospects increases rather than decreases because you've built a system for that, too.

You work "in" your business every day. Invest the time to work "on" your business. As I said previously, you can do it now or you can do it later but sooner or later it must be done. I wish you much luck and success.

Bibliography

"20 Inspirational Quotes From Jim Rohn." *Habits for Well-Being.* Accessed April 19, 2020. https://www.habitsforwellbeing.com/20-inspirational-quotes-from-jim-rohn/.

Anspach, Dana. "U.S. Stock Bear Markets And Their Subsequent Recoveries." *The Balance.* March 20, 2020. https://www.thebalance.com/u-s-stock-bear-markets-and-their-subsequent-recoveries-2388520.

"Babybust? Only 11.7% of financial advisors are under 35: Cerulli." *The Retirement Income Journal.* March 8, 2018. https://retirementincomejournal.com/article/babybust-only-11-7-of-financial-advisors-are-under-35-cerulli/.

"Fall Down 7 Times, Get Up 8." *Mental Toughness Partners.* September 2, 2018. https://www.mentaltoughnesspartners.com/fall-down-seven-times-get-up-eight/.

Foster, Jennifer. "Whether You Think You Can Or Whether You Think You Can't, You're Right." *Wall Street Insanity.* Accessed April 19, 2020.

https://wallstreetinsanity.com/whether-you-think-you-can-or-whether-you-think-you-cant-youre-right/.

Henton, Will. "High Earners, Not Rich Yet (HENRYs)." *Investopedia.* Updated April 6, 2019. https://www.investopedia.com/terms/h/high-earners-not-yet-rich-henrys.asp.

Hicks, Grant. "Why 85% of Financial Advisors Don't Do Feedback." *LinkedIn Pulse.* May 29, 2017. https://www.linkedin.com/pulse/why-85-financial-advisors-dont-do-feedback-grant-hicks/.

"I Have not Failed. I've Just 10,000 Ways It Won't Work." *Mr. Great Motivation.* Accessed August 1, 2020. https://www.mrgreatmotivation.com/2017/12/i-have-not-failed-i-have-just-found.html.

Kitces, Michael. "3 Reasons Why The Financial Advisor Market Sized Isn't Actually Shrinking." *Kitces Nerd's Eye View.* November 15, 2018. https://www.kitces.com/blog/financial-advisor-headcount-total-addressable-market-tam-technology-hiring-growth/.

Kitces, Michael. "Assessing Compatibility To Partner With Another Financial Advisor." July 11, 2016. https://www.kitces.com/blog/financial-advisor-partner-compatibility-assessment-from-partnership-resource/.

Li, Yun. "Wall Street's Fear Gauge Closes At Its Highest Level Ever, Surpassing Even Financial Crisis

Peak." *CNBC,* March 16, 2020. https://www.cnbc.com/2020/03/16/wall-streets-fear-gauge-hits-highest-level-ever.html.

Mullen Jr, David J. "Million Dollar Financial Advisor Team." Accessed May 17, 2020. https://books.google.com/books?id=J-hWDwAAQBAJ&newbks=0&printsec=frontcover&pg=PA122&dq=strategic+vs.+tactical+financial+advisor+team&hl=en#v=onepage&q=strategic%20vs.%20tactical%20financial%20advisor%20team&f=false.

"Alexander Pope Quotes." *Brain Quote.* Accessed August 1, 2020. https://www.brainyquote.com/quotes/alexander_pope_101451.

Siebert, Al. "The Survivor Personality Chapter 1." *Practical Psychology Press.* Accessed April 18, 2020. https://practicalpsychologypress.com/resources/survivor-personality-chapter-one/.

"Succession Planning for Financial Advisors." *Cuna Mutual Group.* Accessed April 1, 2019. https://www.cunamutual.com/resource-library/insights/operations/succession-planning-for-financial-advisors.

Szalavitz, Maria. "Study: A Simple Surgery Checklist Saves Lives. "*Time.* January 14, 2009.

http://content.time.com/time/health/article/0,8599,18
71759,00.html

ELIAS R. DAU, CRPC®

Elias R. Dau began his career as a financial advisor in 1997. Over his two decades in financial services, Elias built his own book of business while also taking on progressive leadership roles. He is most comfortable with a "player coach" leadership style because he has applied most of his leadership concepts to his own practice as a successful financial advisor. He is always willing to spend time with advisors and their clients or prospects.

Elias started his career in the New York City area and has been an individual producer as well as a team producer. After graduating early from a rigorous training program at a top wirehouse, he quickly became the leader of the training program. With a "worst to first" mentality, he and his team were able to take their local program to first place in the country and keep it there.

Having a track record of success, Elias was given additional responsibilities as a producing Sales Manager and then a Director role in New Jersey. In this capacity, he successfully merged two large offices, in the midst of the financial crisis of 2008, and helped financial advisors keep their businesses thriving through the toughest economic cycle of their entire careers.

In 2014, Elias moved his family to Southern California to run a large wirehouse office. He was able to take advantage of the affluent local market and helped his advisors become and stay successful. In this capacity, Elias managed over 200 high-performing financial professionals and took his office to the top five position in the country.

Elias has since left the wirehouse world and has a leadership role, in Southern California, at a Fortune 500 firm. He enjoys coaching his seasoned advisors, developing his new advisors and helping them strive to be better and to better serve their clients.

Elias is married to Tracy and they have three fantastic children. Elias and his family live a busy lifestyle in Southern California where Tracy works in the emergency room at the local hospital. In her spare time she volunteers for the parent support group at their children's school while Elias volunteers as a soccer referee in a youth soccer league. They all enjoy spending time outside together biking, snow skiing, fishing, camping and playing at the beach.

www.eliasrdau.com
me@eliasrdau.com

Made in the USA
Las Vegas, NV
28 December 2021